PRIMARY SCIENCE
TAKING THE PLUNGE
SECOND EDITION

Wynne Harlen

with chapters by
Jos Elstgeest and Sheila Jelly

HEINEMANN • Portsmouth, NH

Heinemann

361 Hanover Street
Portsmouth, NH 03801–3912
www.heinemann.com

Offices and agents throughout the world

The author and publisher wish to thank those who have generously given permission to reprint borrowed material:

Figure 5–2 is reprinted from the *SPACE Research Report: Growth* by T. J. Russell and D. Watt. Copyright © 1990. Reprinted by permission of Liverpool University Press, Liverpool, England.

Figure 5–4 is reprinted from the *SPACE Research Report: Light* by J. Osborne, P. Black, M. Smith, and J. Meadows. Copyright © 1990. Reprinted by permission of Liverpool University Press, Liverpool, England.

Figure 5–8 is reprinted from *Concept Cartoons in Science Education* by S. Naylor and B. Keogh. Copyright © 2000. Reprinted by permission of Millgate House Publishers, Sandbach, England.

Library of Congress Cataloging-in-Publication Data
Harlen, Wynne.
    Primary science : taking the plunge / Wynne Harlen with chapters by Jos Elstgeest and Sheila Jelly.—2nd ed.
        p. cm.
    Includes bibliographical references and index.
    ISBN 0-325-00386-6 (alk. paper)
    1. Science—Study and teaching (Elementary). 2. Interaction analysis in education. I. Elstgeest, Jos. II. Jelly, Sheila. III. Title.

LB1585 .P75 2001
372.3'5044—dc21

2001039343

Editor: Robin Najar
Production: Vicki Kasabian
Cover design: Jenny Jensen Greenleaf
Manufacturing: Steve Bernier

Printed in the United States of America on acid-free paper
12 11 10 09 08   VP   11 12 13 14

The book is dedicated to the memory of Jos Elstgeest, inspired science educator and originator of the phrase "taking the plunge," and to the memory of Roger Osborne, whose research into children's ideas opened many eyes to children's thinking in science.

Contents

Acknowledgments

The original *Taking the Plunge* was the product of a small group of science educators from different countries sharing their particular experiences in helping teachers with the *how* of teaching science to children in the five- to thirteen-year-old age range. The longevity of the first edition pays tribute not only to the continued importance of the teacher's role but also to the perception of the authors in identifying and addressing teachers' key concerns. In revising and updating the book, I have aimed to maintain the original direct relevance to matters of questioning; taking account of children's own ideas; encouraging children to observe, to plan and conduct investigations, and to communicate their findings; and assessing children's progress. I have left essentially unchanged two chapters, one by Jos Elstgeest and one by Sheila Jelly. Those by Roger Osborne and David Symington have been substantially revised but their writing has informed the revision and I would like to acknowledge their continued presence in this book.

Introduction

This book has not been revised since it was first published in 1985. In the intervening time there have been many books and schemes written to give teachers ideas for classroom activities and to provide background knowledge in science. Yet the fact that *Taking the Plunge* has been reprinted many times and has a widespread readership in many countries testifies to its continuing relevance to teachers and others concerned with teaching science at the primary-school level. (Primary is equivalent to elementary, meaning the period of education up to the age of twelve.) The reason may well be because the book is about the teacher's role and aims to give help with the teacher's activities and understanding of children's learning in science. For even at this time, when computers are making great changes in the sources of information and the range of evidence available to children, the role of the teacher remains as central as ever to learning. Teachers will continue, regularly if not daily, to be faced with questions such as:

- How do I encourage children to interact with and learn about and from the things around them?
- What do I do if they don't explore things or observe carefully?
- What do I do if they don't ask questions?
- How do I answer the questions that they do ask?
- What do I do if their ideas are not consistent with scientific ideas?
- How do I help them to plan and carry out investigations in a scientific manner?
- How do I ensure that they learn from activities?
- How do I know if they are learning?

It is with these questions that this book is concerned. It is not comprehensive in covering everything relevant to the teaching of primary science; there is nothing about choosing and organizing equipment, nor about managing science at the school level, nor about medium-

and long-term planning for science. Other publications cover these topics (e.g., ASE 1998; Harlen 2000b; Harlen and Jelly 1997). Instead it is the aim here to help with the daily interactions among the children, teacher, and materials—interactions that make all the difference as to whether children's activities are genuine learning experiences.

Since the early 1980s an expansion of research into young children's learning in science has led to better understanding of the learning process, the formation of children's ideas, and the kinds of experience that promote development of scientific concepts and process skills. There is a great deal that we yet have to learn about these things, but current understanding suggests that the key aspects of the teacher's role continue to be: asking and answering questions, encouraging children to ask questions and answer them through inquiry, enabling children to make their ideas and reasoning explicit through communication, and supporting development of science process skills, concepts, and attitudes. In addition, it has been recognized that considerable advances in learning follow when teachers use assessment formatively. This means gathering and using, during teaching, information about children's developing ideas and skills, sharing this with children as feedback on how they can improve their learning, and involving them in assessing their own progress. The rationale for the choice of chapters in this book is, therefore, that they focus on these central aspects of the teacher's role in children's learning.

The extent to which the material has been revised or rewritten varies in different chapters. Two chapters—one by Jos Elstgeest on "The Right Question at the Right Time" (Chapter 3) and one by Sheila Jelly on "Helping Children to Raise Questions—and Answering Them" (Chapter 4)—have been left untouched. These chapters have stood the test of time and are as enlightening in their direct and relevant messages today as when they were written almost twenty years ago. Other chapters have been largely rewritten, bringing the material up to date but, I hope, preserving the original pertinence, usefulness, and clarity through extensive use of examples. The final chapter, on formative assessment, is entirely new. As before, each chapter concludes with a summary of its main points and lists suggestions for action that teachers might take.

Chapter Outlines

Chapter 1: Why Science? What Science?

This chapter is concerned with the why? what? and how? questions about primary science. *Why* is answered in terms of the importance of building understanding of the scientific aspects of the children's environment through developing and using skills of inquiry that will enable learning to continue throughout life. A further answer comes from the well-established fact that children develop ideas about these scientific aspects whether or not they are taught science, but that these ideas will often be nonscientific and can interfere with later learning, providing an obvious role for primary school science. *What* is answered by suggesting the process skills, concept areas, and attitudes that are relevant as goals for learning science at the primary level. *How* is answered by suggesting a sequence of steps that describe the process of inquiry and lead to a framework for learning through inquiry that provides a link with the later chapters.

Chapter 2: Bringing Children and Science Together

As the title suggests, this chapter is about setting the scene for children to learn through inquiry. An important aim is for children to be motivated to learn because of the satisfaction that this way of learning brings. This means being intrinsically motivated, as opposed to extrinsically motivated, which happens when learning is undertaken for external reward, such prizes or good grades, rather than for its own sake. This is important because extrinsic motivation encourages surface learning rather than learning with understanding. This chapter discusses the teacher's role in establishing a climate where children enjoy learning. It emphasizes the importance of teachers helping children to value evidence and accepting as the "right" answer the one that fits the evidence available to a child, rather than forcing children to try to understand a more scientifically correct answer for which they have no evidence yet.

Chapter 3: The Right Question at the Right Time

This chapter, by Jos Elstgeest, is about "right" and "wrong" teachers' questions. In this context "right" means that the questions are effective in encouraging inquiry, and so the author also describes them as "productive." The reverse is the case for "wrong" or "unproductive" questions. Later in the chapter, Jos also offers advice to teachers in handling children's "why" questions and gives some suggestions that Sheila Jelly takes further in the next chapter. This chapter is reproduced essentially as it was in the first edition.

Chapter 4: Helping Children Raise Questions—and Answering Them

In this chapter, Sheila Jelly takes up the matter of how to help children ask "productive" questions, ones that lead to investigations that the children can undertake. Her suggestions include establishing a climate that encourages questions, giving time for raising questions, and providing materials that stimulate curiosity. She then provides important advice on how to handle the questions that children ask. A key point is developing the technique of turning "difficult" questions into starting points for inquiry.

Chapter 5: Taking Children's Own Ideas Seriously

The first part of this chapter provides evidence of the ideas that children form from their early experience and thinking. These examples illustrate the common characteristics of children's own ideas and suggest ways to help children toward more scientific ideas. There is also a discussion of ways in which the teacher can gain access to children's ideas, which is relevant in the context of formative assessment (Chapter 9), as well as in the discussion in this chapter of strategies for helping children develop their ideas.

Chapter 6: Helping Children to Plan and Interpret Investigations

Planning and carrying out investigations encompasses all process skills, from raising questions through to reporting conclusions. However, other chapters deal with questioning, observing, and communicating skills, so the focus here is on planning, particularly manipulating and controlling variables and interpreting findings. Not all investigations are of the "fair testing" type and other kinds are discussed and exemplified. Ways of helping children to plan, including the use of a planning board, are brought together at the end of the chapter.

Chapter 7: Helping Children to Observe

Observation is used in all types of investigations and at various points from initial exploration to gathering evidence more systematically, including measurement. This chapter considers the complex nature of observation—which is far more than taking in information through the senses—and its importance in concept formation through detecting patterns, similarities and differences, and other links between objects and phenomena. The role that teachers can play in developing this skill includes providing time and opportunity, equipment for extending the senses, using sense probes and computer data logging, and discussion.

Chapter 8: Helping Children to Communicate

Communication in learning is a vast subject and this chapter focuses on just three forms of communication: discussion; using notebooks or journals; and representation in drawings, paintings, and modeling. In all these forms the benefit is that the act of communicating requires the children to make explicit to themselves, as well as others, their ideas and reasoning. Communication is therefore often a learning experience in its own right, as well as providing the teacher with evidence of what children have achieved and where they are in development. However, communication will not serve these purposes automatically, and the chapter provides suggestions for what the teacher can do to create the atmosphere and set up the situations that enable children to communicate freely.

Chapter 9: Assessing for Learning

This chapter is primarily concerned with formative assessment, that is, using assessment as part of teaching to help learning. The nature and purpose of summative assessment are also discussed, noting that using test results for high-stakes purposes can have a narrowing effect on the curriculum. The powerful potential of formative assessment for advancing learning can be realized only when teachers gather evidence of children's ideas and skills and use this evidence both to adapt their teaching and to give the children suggestions for their next steps in learning and how to take them. Sharing goals with children and involving them in assessing their progress are also key components of formative assessment.

Chapter 1

Why Science? What Science?

As we have said in the introduction, this book is about the practicalities of everyday interactions in science activities in the classroom. Advice at the practical level always derives from people's judgments about what and how children ought to be learning. These judgments, in turn, follow from a view of the nature of science and its role in education. Why are we teaching science at the presecondary stage and what kind of science is most appropriate? Answers to these questions are implicit throughout the chapters of this book, but in this first chapter, we review why it is important for children to learn science and what and how it is important for them to learn from the time they enter school to the age of eleven or twelve years.

Why Science?

Learning science helps children to develop understanding of and ways of understanding the world around them. For this they have to build up concepts that help them link their experiences together and to learn ways of collecting and organizing information and of applying and testing ideas. This learning not only contributes to children's ability to make better sense of things around them, but also prepares them to deal more effectively with wider decision making and problem solving in their lives. For this reason learning science is as basic a part of education as is developing numeracy and literacy. It daily becomes more important as the complexity of technology increases and touches every part of our lives.

So learning science involves processes of thinking and action, and the product can be knowledge of both the process skills involved

1

and a set of scientific ideas or concepts. The processes of science provide ways of finding out information, testing ideas, and seeking explanations; the scientific ideas help in making sense of new experiences. The word *can* is used advisedly here; there is the potential for science activities to have these benefits but no guarantee that they will be realized without taking the appropriate steps.

In learning science, the use and development of processes and concepts must go hand in hand; they cannot be separated. Using process skills on trivial or nonscientific content, where no understanding is developed, is not science. There can be no "content-free" activity that develops science process skills, for without being used on scientific content, the processes are not scientific processes.

Many of the same processes—hypothesizing, predicting, finding out, interpreting data—are used in relation to other subject matter, particularly in social subjects. It is only when they are used on the subject matter of science that they are *science process skills*. Similarly, attempts to develop scientific ideas without the use of process skills leads only to rote learning and knowledge that is confined to the situations in which it was learned, making little contribution to understanding new experiences. In other words, content without processes does not lead to learning with understanding, which, by definition, is knowledge that can be applied in situations other than those in which it was learned.

This interdependence of processes and concepts has important implications for the kinds of activities children need to encounter in their education and for the teacher's role. Before pursuing these implications, there are still two further points to make that underline the value of including science in the education of children from the start.

The first point is that, whether we teach children science or not, they will be developing ideas about the world around them from their earliest years. Incontrovertible evidence from research shows this (see Chapter 5). If these ideas are based on casual observation, noninvestigated events, and the acceptance of hearsay, then they are likely to be nonscientific, "everyday" ideas. There are plenty of such ideas around for children to pick up. For example, my mother believed that the sun shining onto a fire would put it out, that cheese maggots (a common encounter in her youth when food was sold unwrapped) are made of cheese and develop spontaneously from it, that electricity travels more easily if the wires are not twisted. Similar myths still abound, many in advertising slogans, and they no doubt influence children's attempts to make sense of their experience.

As well as picking up ideas from hearsay, left to themselves, children will form some ideas that seem unscientific. For example, they often conclude from their observations that to make something move requires a force, but that it will stop moving without a force acting, that rust comes from within metals, that heavy things sink and light ones float. All these ideas, and the ones learned from hearsay, could easily be tested rather than accepted. Children's science education should make them want to do just that and should provide them with the skills to do it. Then they have the chance not only to modify their ideas, but also to learn to be skeptical about so-called truths until there is evidence to support them. Eventually they will realize that all ideas are working hypotheses (provisional explanations) which can never be proved "right," but are useful as long as they fit the evidence of experience and experiment.

The importance of beginning this learning early in children's education is twofold. On the one hand, the children begin to realize that to be useful ideas must fit the evidence; on the other hand, they are less likely to form and to accept everyday ideas that can be shown to be in conflict with evidence and scientific concepts. There are research findings to show that the longer the nonscientific ideas have been held, the more difficult they are to change. Many children come to secondary science not merely lacking the scientific ideas they need, but possessing alternative ideas that are a barrier to understanding their science lessons (Osborne and Freyberg 1982, 1985).

The second point about starting to learn science, and to learn scientifically, at the primary level is connected with attitudes to the subject. There is evidence that attitudes to science seem to be formed earlier than attitudes to most other subjects and children tend to have taken a definite position with regard to their liking of the subject by the age of eleven or twelve (Ormerod and Duckworth 1975). This may well be because science developments and applications generally have a higher profile in the media than news of activities in history or geography. If, in addition, children's early experiences of science are confusing to them because their own ideas are different from what they are taught, it is not surprising that they develop negative attitudes towards it. Science is seen as difficult to learn and not connected with the sense they make of the things in their experience. Such influences undoubtedly affect their later performance and willingness to continue learning in science in the secondary school. Although there is a lesson here for secondary school science, it is clear that much can be done through effective science education at the primary level to avoid this crisis at the primary/secondary interface.

What Science?

Science education begins for children when they realize that they can find things out for themselves by their own actions: by sifting through a handful of sand, by blowing bubbles, by putting salt in water, by comparing different materials, by regular observation of the moon and stars. The ideas they have at the start of such activities may be changed as a result of what they do, what they see, and how they interpret what happens. So the kind of science we are talking about concerns basic ideas that can be developed through simple investigations of objects and materials around them, assisted by information from various sources and by discussion. What ideas emerge from these activities will depend not only on the events but also on the way the children reason about them and process the information, that is, on their process skills.

Individual process skills are identified in slightly different ways in different curricula and standards statements. However, they have much in common and most include the processes in Box 1 in these or similar words:

Box 1
- Observing (including measuring)
- Raising questions (distinguishing between investigable and noninvestigable ones)
- Hypothesizing (proposing possible explanations)

- Predicting (saying what may happen on the basis of a hypothesis)
- Planning and carrying out investigations (including fair testing)
- Interpreting information obtained (pattern finding, inferring, drawing conclusions)
- Communicating (recording, reporting, discussing)

These can be grouped in various ways. For example, in the English national curriculum they are put under the headings of "planning," "obtaining and presenting evidence," and "considering evidence and evaluating." In the National Science Education Standards they are grouped under the headings "identify questions that can be answered through scientific investigation," "design and conduct a scientific investigation," "use appropriate tools and techniques to gather, analyze, and interpret data," "develop descriptions, explanations, predictions, and models, using evidence," and "think critically and logically to make the relationships between evidence and explanations."

Some process skills fall into more than one of these categories and so exact classification is not possible, nor is it really relevant. The value lies in drawing attention to the importance of going beyond simply gathering information to trying to understand it and then testing out the new ideas that emerge. In this way the ideas the children develop are their own, ones that arise from their own thinking and not from someone else's view of the world.

Of course, the purpose of science education is to enable children to develop ideas about the world around them that fit evidence and so are shared by others; that is, what we call "the scientific view of things." The key to effective science teaching is to enable children to develop this view for themselves, not to impose it as the "right" answer. But what ideas are we talking about? From the points made so far it follows that they should be ideas that

- help children to understand everyday events and their experience of the world

- are within their grasp, taking into account their limited and developing experience and ways of thinking
- are accessible to and testable by children through the use of process skills
- provide a foundation for further science education and the development of scientific literacy

It is important to keep these criteria in mind in reviewing any list of content, since in all cases the ideas can be developed at a range of levels from simple to sophisticated. The list in Box 2 covers what is included in most curricula or standards.

Box 2

- Living things and the processes of life (characteristics of living things, how they are made up and the functions of their parts, reproduction and heredity, regulation, human health, etc.)
- The interaction of living things and their environment (competition, diversity, adaptation, effects of pollution, and other human activities, etc.)
- Materials (their variety, properties, sources, uses, interactions, conservation, disposal of waste, etc.)
- Air, atmosphere, and weather (presence of air around the Earth; features of the weather; causes of clouds, rain, frost, and snow; freak conditions; etc.)
- Structure and history of the Earth (rocks, soil, and materials from the Earth; maintenance of soil fertility; fossil fuels, minerals, and ores as limited resources)
- The Earth in space (sun, moon, stars, and planets; causes of day and night and seasonal variations)
- Forces and movement (starting and stopping movement, speed and acceleration, simple machines, transportation, etc.)
- Energy sources and uses (sources of heat, light, sound, electricity, etc.)
- Science and technology in society (some of the history and nature of science and technology and how they influence society)

Other important outcomes of children's science activities come under the heading of attitudes. Attitudes to science were mentioned earlier (page 3) as part of the reasons for giving children experience of genuine scientific activities in order for them to form informed attitudes relating to science. However, equally important are attitudes *of* science; attitudes relating to the process of activity of scientific inquiry, for example those included in Box 3:

attitudes

Box 3
- Curiosity (wanting to raise questions and to find out answers)
- Respect for evidence (willingness to gather and take account of evidence to test ideas)
- Open-mindedness (willingness to change ideas in the light of evidence)
- Critical reflection (willingness to review the implications of new ideas and evidence for how things previously encountered were understood)
- Sensitivity to the living and nonliving environment (avoiding harm to the subjects of investigation)

It is not difficult to see that these attitudes influence the use and development of process skills and so are important goals of science education. It is equally evident that their formation is highly dependent on the way in which science is taught.

How?

To decide what experiences we want to give children in order to achieve the goals of developing process skills, attitudes, and ideas, we have to consider the way children learn and their experience at different stages. "Understanding the world around" means different things for a five-year-old, a nine-year-old, a thirteen-year-old, and so on, because their capacities for understanding are different and so are their worlds. The ideas of a young child will be those that fit his or her limited world. They will have to be modified and extended to fit expanding experience and capacity for understanding. Likewise a child's skills, both mental and physical, will develop. For instance, skill in observing will progress from making observations of the most obvious similarities and differences that are nondiscriminating (but right for the purposes of a young child) to paying attention to the detail and relevance of what is observed (again right for children with a greater range of experience).

School activities must take into account the way children learn at the primary level, when thinking and doing are closely related. Understanding depends on children working things out for themselves. It's important to note that this is not the same as saying that everything has to be learned from scratch or from firsthand interaction. What it does mean is that children should be able to be satisfied that the ideas they accept fit the evidence as far as they can tell. Some of these ideas may have been developed by the children themselves, or may have been offered by other children, by their teacher, or found in a book. In all cases the ideas must be related to evidence, subjected to critical examination, and modified or reconstructed, if necessary, in the light of evidence. This is where the process skills come in—to gather and interpret information, to devise and carry out fair tests and other kinds of investigations, and to communicate results.

So learning activities must allow process skills, attitudes, and concepts to develop together. That is why emphasis is laid on how children learn and not just on what they learn. A particular activity could be carried out by some children just following instructions as in a recipe, and by other children thinking their way through from step to step. The difference is created by what the teacher does in preparation for, and during, the activity. Keeping children busy, physically active, is not the criterion for effective science teaching. Activity must be a vehicle for experience and thought, and thought is promoted by communication and discussion. The teacher's role in this process is crucial to children's learning.

It may be helpful to have in mind an overview of how learning in science can take place. How, in other words, they can move a few steps toward the scientific view (as defined above) from their initial ideas, which may not be based on evidence but on first impressions or hearsay. Generally this is a gradual progression, and we don't expect children to leap to a full understanding of an idea all at once.

Children bring to new experiences not empty minds ready to be filled with new information, but ideas picked up or created from their past encounters and from the links they have made between the old and new experiences (see Chapter 5). It is the same for all learners, and children are not special in this respect. We all try to relate what we already know to a new experience in order to start making sense of it. The main difference between children and adults is in the range of experience and existing ideas available to help in making sense of the new. For example, I have often seen children try to explain the moisture that forms on the outside of a cold can when ice is placed inside it in terms of water from the ice leaking through from inside. This is a reasonable explanation, based on the idea that the moisture must have come from the only place where there seems to be water—if you have no idea that there is water vapor in the air that can condense on cold surfaces. How might they be helped toward a different and more scientific explanation?

The first thing is to take this idea seriously; it is a reasonable hypothesis that can be tested. The testing might go something like this:

If it is water leaking through, then we shouldn't find the moisture outside if the inside of the ice is, say, wrapped in something that the children agree does not let water through and the can is dry inside.	The hypothesis is used to make a prediction
Then the children decide what to do to see if there is moisture outside when the ice is wrapped up.	The prediction is tested through an investigation
The result of the investigation provides evidence to show that the prediction is incorrect; there is still moisture on the cold parts of the can.	The results are used to reach a conclusion about the hypothesis
Is there another explanation? Other ideas are considered.	Return to the first step and use a different hypothesis to make a new prediction.

9

Sometimes the cycle is passed through very quickly, perhaps as a "thought experiment" rather than an actual experiment. An adult might well reason in this way and go immediately to an alternative explanation. In each cycle, there is learning—even if the prediction is not supported by the evidence. The concept involved becomes better defined by being tested in a new situation. When the evidence does fit the prediction and so supports the hypothesis, the underlying idea is strengthened. So if the children suggest that the moisture must come from the air around (because they have seen cold surfaces in the bathroom "mist over" when they take a hot shower, for example) then their idea about moisture in the air is enlarged and they begin to understand that it is there although they can't see it. However, even in this simple example, we see that the outcome depends not only on the initial idea but on how it is tested; that is, on the processes (of hypothesizing, predicting, interpreting, and so on) and how they were carried out.

By generalizing, we arrive at a framework for describing learning through inquiry. We should include the first two steps evident in the example—of identifying a question that can be answered through investigation and of using evidence from earlier experience to create a possible explanation. So the complete sequence becomes as in Figure 1–1.

In the rest of this book we look at the teacher's role in the various parts of the learning process described in Figure 1–1. Chapter 2 is about getting started and setting up the situations and classroom atmosphere that motivates this kind of learning. Chapters 3 and 4 are concerned with helping children to raise questions that are productive in focusing this kind of learning, and with handling the range of questions of all kinds that children will ask. Chapter 5 provides some examples and insight into the ideas that children are likely to have formed from their earlier experience and will bring to the classroom. It also identifies the teacher's role in bringing children into contact with ideas different from their own. Chapter 6 suggests some ways in which the teacher can help children to plan, carry out investigations, and interpret the results of their investigations. Then we have Chapter 7, about helping children to gather evidence for developing their ideas through observation, which is relevant at all stages, from the initial

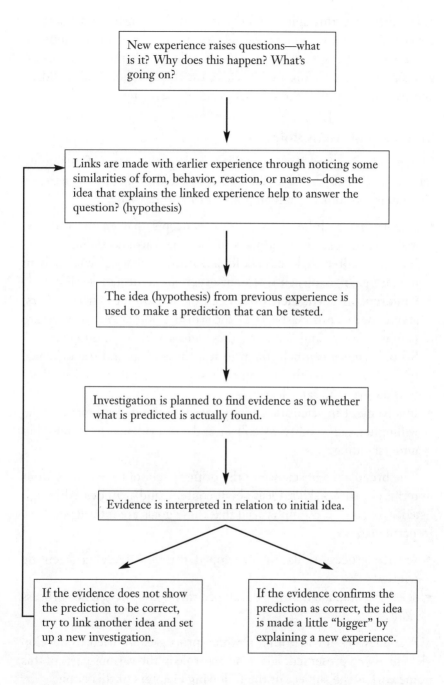

Figure 1–1. *A framework for learning through inquiry*

new experience through to completing an investigation. Chapter 8 concerns communication, which also has a central role throughout the process of learning through inquiry. Finally, in Chapter 9 we discuss assessment, emphasizing its formative use in providing both children and teacher with information that promotes learning.

Summary of Main Points

In this chapter we have reviewed briefly the case of including science as part of the basic education of children in the primary, or elementary, school. The main points made were that

- Science helps children to develop concepts that enable them to make sense of scientific aspects of the world around them.
- It helps children to develop skills and attitudes that will enable them to continue making sense of their experiences throughout life.
- Children will form their own ideas, or pick up ideas from others, about the scientific aspects of the world whether or not they are taught science, and many of these ideas will be "nonscientific." School science can help them to test these ideas and use evidence to modify or reject them at an early stage so that they are less likely to interfere with later learning.
- Involvement in scientific activity can help the development of the willingness and ability to collect and use evidence in developing understanding.

The broad aims of science in the primary school have been set out in terms of process skills, ideas about content, and attitudes. Although listed separately, it is emphasized that these goals are interdependent. In particular,

- science process skills are developed through studying scientific content
- scientific understanding is developed through using science process skills.

A framework for learning in which processes are used to develop ideas has been presented. The teacher's role in the various parts of this framework is the subject of the following chapters of this book.

Chapter 2

Bringing Children and Science Together

In the first edition of this book the second chapter, written by Jos Elstgeest and titled "Encounter, Interaction, and Dialogue" began with this story:

> Tiny Niels, beaming, bare and beautiful, crawled on the wet sand of the beach. He moved where the sea reaches out for the land, where the ocean barely touches the continent, where the exhausted waves drag themselves up the incline and withdraw or sink into the sand. Whenever this happened in slow and steady rhythm there appeared, all around Niels, tiny holes in the sand which bubbled and boiled with escaping air. These little marvels drew his attention, and with immense concentration he poked his finger in hole after hole, until a fresh wave wiped them all out and created new ones. Then Niels' game would start anew, until an unexpectedly powerful wave of the incoming tide knocked him over and, frightened, he gave up his play and cried.
>
> Witnessing such a simple encounter between child and world places all our well-learned treatises on child development and on the child's orientation in this world in the shadow. Here on this beach it happened. This was it. And we, adult know-alls, have nothing to add. The bubbling holes invited Niels: "Come here, look at us, feel and poke." And Niels did exactly that. He could not talk yet, not a word was exchanged, no question was formulated, but the boy himself was the question, a living query: "What is this? What does it do? How does it feel?"
>
> Question and answer converge here, flow together. The query of the child is the response to the challenge of the thing, of the bubbling holes. And the question coming from Niels as well as the answer he seeks and gets, passes through the same probing finger. A perfect interaction. Who dares interfere?

> Countless such encounters occur in the lives of little people. Daily
> they meet with something new out of their world, and every time
> there is the invitation, the urge for interaction and dialogue: "Look at
> me, feel me, handle me, try me, smell me, sniff me, lick me, taste me,
> hear me."
>
> It may be the clouds in the sky, or the birds in the undergrowth; it
> may be a bumblebee on the clover, or a spider in a web, the pollen of a
> flower, or the ripples in a pond. It may be the softness of a fleece, the
> "bang!!" in a drum, or the rainbow in a soap film. From all around
> comes the invitation; all around sounds the challenge. The question is
> there, the answer lies hidden, and the child has the key.

Here we have an almost poetic account of engagement between a
child and everyday phenomena, beautifully illustrating the natural
curiosity that creates and drives the desire to learn. But the account
was followed by two questions that shake one out of any assumption
that this romantic view of learning has much in common with what
takes place in formal education: "Is this image, this interplay, this
encounter between child and object, child and world clearly recog-
nizable in the school? Is it obvious in your school, in your class with
your own children?"

Clearly there has to be a big difference between the informal exploration by one child in close contact with the natural environment and
the activities of children as part of a class in school. However, there
are elements of the informal encounter that are highly relevant to
learning in any situation and that we would want to preserve. What
are these and how can we be sure that they are present in what we do
to help elementary school children learn science? Some of the most
important points, relating to motivation for learning and ownership
over it, the use of evidence and the atmosphere that encourages
inquiry and experimentation, are considered in this chapter.

Motivation for Learning

All learning is motivated in one way or another, but there are
different kinds of motivation. One can be motivated by the sheer
interest and enjoyment of finding out what happens, as was baby
Niels. One can also be motivated by fear of punishment or desire for
rewards, as happens when children are told off or have their freedom

restricted if they don't perform as expected, or when their efforts are directed at achieving a "gold star" or special praise from the teacher. Again, one can be motivated by wanting to be "the best" or "top of the class," or by wanting to avoid being at the bottom of the class.

The first of these is often called *intrinsic* motivation. It means that there is satisfaction in learning, in what is learned and in the way of engaging with it. If there is intrinsic motivation for a task, a learner will persist with it, engage in further learning and not be satisfied until it is understood. There is evidence from research that intrinsically motivated learning leads to higher levels of achievement and to what is often described as "deep," as opposed to "surface" learning (Deci and Ryan 1985). It contrasts with the second type of motivation, called *extrinsic*, which means that learners engage in their tasks mainly because of external incentives. Giving rewards for learning encourages extrinsic motivation and leads to learning that is undertaken as quickly as possible and with the minimum effort to gain the reward, whether it is praise or privilege, or just passing a test. Not surprisingly, this tends to encourage shallow or "surface" learning, such as committing things to memory without understanding—and forgetting them soon after the test has been passed or the reward obtained. The third type of motivation, called *achievement* motivation (McMeniman 1989), produces those who strive hard to be at the top and succeed by sheer effort; they find their reward in comparing themselves with others. But it also leads to some who coast along, doing just enough to avoid failure and never stretching themselves.

Why are different kinds of motivation important in learning? Those who study this aspect of learning suggest that it is related to the feeling of being in control of one's understanding. Giving rewards for learning puts the control of learning in the hands of those who give the rewards. The learner has to match up to the standards that others set rather than his or her own internalized standards. It is not difficult to see that once a learner loses the feeling of being in control, of knowing what he or she is trying to learn, and of working out what to do and why, it becomes necessary to follow the directions and requirements of others. The motivation becomes "if you do this, I will give you _____" rather than "if I do this, I will learn _____." In conditions of extrinsic motivation, children may learn by rote but are less likely to learn conceptually. Praise is a form of reward that has to be used discriminately if it is not to lose its effect. It makes children feel good, particularly if the praise is directed at the effort rather than the product. But praise alone will not advance children's learning. They also need to know how to direct this effort (see also Chapter 9, page 129).

From these arguments it follows that, for learning in science particularly, where the aim is to develop *understanding* of things around and not just surface knowledge, intrinsic motivation is desirable if not essential. But children often have to do things they don't choose to do and to learn things that they don't find intrinsically interesting. What then? Before answering this, let's look at the conditions that promote intrinsic motivation.

- First is the importance of some challenge in the activities from which children are intended to learn, a challenge that provides the incentive to "want to know." The environment of children is rich with such opportunities. Take the study of water—what will float? What will sink? How can a floating object be made to sink and vice versa? How can water be made to move, upwards as well as downwards? What happens when water freezes? What happens when it boils? How can you stop ice melting? And so on and so on. These are only a tiny fraction of the questions that children can raise and try to answer by inquiry—and these are just the questions about water. Of course a challenge is only a challenge if it is something you have not done before. And it is not a challenge if you already know the answer—so baking buns with and without yeast to see what difference it makes is not a challenge if you know that buns need yeast to make them rise. It is a pity, when there is so much to explore, to spend time on things that are frequently found in teacher's guides but do not provide a real opportunity for children to advance their ideas.

- Second, providing some choice in the matter of what question to pursue and how to go about it ensures some commitment to undertake an activity and carry it through. So the teacher who involves children in identifying the aspect of a topic that they want to investigate, in deciding on their goal in an activity, and in choosing what they are going to do to work toward it will be increasing the intrinsic motivation of the experience and hence the learning.

- Third, challenging experiences often produce problems, and children need constructive feedback to help them over such problems. Here it should not be just the teacher's view of the problem and how to solve it, but the children can also be involved in assessing what they have done and what they need to do to overcome the problem. We have more to say about children being involved in self-assessment in Chapter 9.
- Fourth, cooperative learning promotes intrinsic motivation, so setting up activities in ways that promote genuine collaboration—not children being physically placed next to each other but essentially working independently—will ensure that there is a collective responsibility for the work and that each child needs to play his or her part in it.
- Fifth, it is important to provide some feedback that supports high expectations and the confidence that the children will succeed. It sets up a "virtuous circle" in which children try harder and as a result succeed, which raises their self-esteem and confidence as learners. This will be all the more easily established where the activity interests the children so that they have the incentive to persevere.

All of these points indicate that the children have acquired some ownership of the activity, which will have the effect of engaging their thinking and effort because it is theirs and they understand what they have to do and why. This is so different from working from a set of instructions produced by someone else, when the reasons for what has to be done may not be obvious or understood. The same arguments for ensuring intrinsic motivation and ownership can be used to identify situations and actions to be avoided if we want to encourage the improved learning that these things can bring. Things to avoid will include

- making comparisons between children so that they are encouraged to compete with each other rather than cooperate
- having classroom rules that have to be followed slavishly without explaining reasons for them or giving children opportunity to take part in deciding them

- making fun—even lightheartedly—of children's work ("That looks more like a sausage than a worm!")
- blaming children for showing lack of interest in activities, especially when they have had no part in choosing them.

So we return to the problem of dealing with the unavoidable situations where things have to be done and learned that are really not all that interesting in themselves. These include learning techniques for measuring and using other equipment, such as lenses and microscopes; taking necessary precautions for the sake of safety or conserving the environment; routine care for animals and plants; and clearing up after messy activities. It's necessary to find ways of motivating learning in these situations without falling into the trap of bribing or threatening with rewards or punishments. It helps in all such cases to explain the reasons for restricting children's freedom to do what they might prefer. "We have to clean out the animal cages/wash our hands/use the hand lens this way, so that _____ ." Children will readily agree if the reason is genuine. There may also be room for some choice even in these matters so that some ownership can be established. A restricted choice is better than having no choice at all or being threatened with punishment if things are not done in the way prescribed.

Use of Evidence

The essence of science is making sense of experience of the real things in the world around us. Science is essentially a human endeavor and the sense that is made of some phenomenon at a certain time depends on both the evidence available at that time and the ability of human beings to develop new ideas or adapt existing ones. Scientific ideas have changed over the years, sometimes because new evidence becomes available to challenge the prevailing ideas, which has often happened through technological change that provides better ways of detecting relevant evidence.

Sometimes new evidence can be accommodated by modifying existing ideas; in other cases new ways of thinking may be needed. New ideas often result from leaps of the imagination and creative thinking that links together events that have not been linked before.

A good example is the story of how Newton is supposed to have linked the fall of an apple from a tree with the force that keeps the moon orbiting the Earth. But all new ideas have then to be tested against evidence if they are to be accepted as scientific. This process is essentially the same as in children's learning—trying to explain an experience and then testing the explanation by seeing if what it predicts is supported by evidence of what actually happens. In this sense learning science and doing science are the same. As an aside, it is a pity that the term "discovery learning" gives the impression that the ideas that explain something are there in the objects of phenomena ready to be revealed. Whereas instead, the objects just provide the evidence for testing the ideas that we create. It is the preeminence of evidence from the real world that distinguishes science from other subjects. For example in mathematics, the test of an idea lies in the logic of numbers and relationships, which do not have to relate to anything in the real world (for example, nonrational numbers).

The "truth" and the "right" answer

Somewhere in the conscience of every teacher lies a sense of duty concerning what is true; we are inclined to think that we ought to present the children with the "right" answer. But it is a mistake to think that we can do this by simply telling them what we believe to be true. Scientific activity, and also the children's activity, is directed toward detecting the answer to a question as it reveals itself in the reality of the things we study. Therefore, we must begin to look for a new kind of "right" answer. We must begin to look for a right answer that the children can give with confidence, that depends on their own observations: a right answer that originates from their experiences. This right answer may fall short of "the truth." In other words, we are concerned with, and interested in, what the searching child finds out, what he or she observes, what he or she thinks and has to say about his or her experiences. The professional scientist, too, would produce his or her experience and his or her evidence in order to corroborate what he or she regards and expresses as true fact. Thus we should not ask children to recite what somebody else thinks, but what they themselves think is true.

The reason for this kind of "right" answer is to help the child to think clearly and independently. Even when we disagree with the child in what the evidence shows—as may well be the case—a blunt "Wrong!" would still be out of place. First of all, we might well be wrong ourselves. Second, "right" and "wrong" do not depend on our authority, but on the authority of the evidence, which the child may not have completely explored. Further observation may well correct the child's original statement.

To illustrate this point Jos Elstgeest related this story:

> When I worked with antlions and children, I found that children at first were convinced that antlions eat dust. [Antlions are insect larvae found in many countries, but not in the U.K., that dig conical holes in loose soil or sand, into which small insects, often ants, fall and become the antlion's prey.] Their fresh experience shows them that an antlion sits at the bottom of a dusty pit for a long time. That the creature patiently waits for some bait, like an ant, to stray into the pit so he can catch and eat it, is not yet part of their experience. What is part of their daily experience, however, is that one should eat in order to stay alive. So, if the antlion lives, he must eat the only thing that seems to be available to him: dust. What happens if we now say to the children, "No, that is wrong"? Naturally, the idea of dry dust being food is absurd to us, but will the children be any happier with our statement? This would only imply that they were wrong in the eyes of the teacher for, at this stage, they have no way of understanding any better. The teacher's authoritative statement has in no way enriched the children's experience of the truth. Further experience, however, is bound to make the children change their mind about what antlions eat. So continue to let the children observe the antlions in action until they have enough evidence to make them change their minds.
>
> Letting the children persist in this obviously faulty opinion was too much for one conscientious teacher. He persuaded the children to go and feed ants to the antlions "so you can see what they really eat." They did this and the teacher contentedly thought: "that settles the mistake." Later, when the teacher looked through the children's notebooks, he found to his amazement that "Antlions eat dust. But if they get an ant, they eat that too." The last bit was a concession to their teacher, for they were just convinced that ants are no more than a welcome supplement to the antlion's dusty diet.

The Classroom Atmosphere

Everything that happens in the classroom takes place within the ethos or social climate created by the teacher. Children have to feel free to express their own ideas and ways of thinking, without fear that they will be giving the "wrong" answer. So before a teacher can have any chance of gaining access to children's thinking, it is necessary to establish a classroom climate in which children feel that it is "safe" to talk freely about their ideas and their work, knowing that what they say is valued, taken seriously, and will not be disregarded or ridiculed. What can a teacher do to establish such a helping classroom atmosphere?

It is important to show real concern for children's feelings and interests just as we do for our friends. The concern has to be genuine; children are not taken in by the superficial interest of the teacher. Sincerity is conveyed not just through words, but also by manner, and particularly by listening to what they have to say.

When teachers have found out about children's attitudes and feelings, they should use this knowledge to set realistic expectations. This means, for instance, recognizing that not all children have reached the same level of maturity in cooperation or responsibility, and some need more support in developing and applying these qualities.

The teacher can set up the classroom organization so that children can take responsibility, appropriate to their maturity, for the materials they use and for completing their work. This has implications for the physical arrangement of materials in the room—so that children have easy access to equipment and can find and replace what they need—and for managing time, so that children can finish their work to their own satisfaction.

Teachers can recognize and encourage effort and socially desirable behaviors, not just achievement. Cooperation, politeness, and thoughtfulness are not just important as social skills but also help to develop a learning community where children are ready to listen to, heed, and learn from each other's ideas. Of course the best way to help children develop these qualities is by example. Moreover, children appreciate these qualities in teachers; they like their teacher to be polite, patient, sympathetic, encouraging, and fair.

In science particularly it is important to foster curiosity and encourage persistence and creativity in satisfying it. Sometimes this takes children into an unintended path that diverts from the aim of the lesson. For example, it can be disconcerting to leave children to explore how corks float on water and then to return to find them fascinated by putting other things in the water. But it is important that the teacher does not intervene immediately to stop them, and instead observes carefully from a distance to see exactly what they are doing and then asks them to explain. More often than not they will have a reason, connected in their thinking with the activity, but not one the teacher had thought of.

An environment that is created in these ways will be one where children can confidently discuss their thinking with a teacher who is interested in it. In turn they will be interested in what the teacher has to contribute to the conversation and to further investigation. They will be ready to assimilate ideas from the teacher, who has become part of, and partner in, their inquiry.

Summary of Main Points

This chapter has been all about setting up the conditions in which children can learn through inquiry, learn to value and use evidence in making sense of what they find, and learn to enjoy learning. In particular we have discussed the teacher's role in creating conditions needed to promote intrinsic motivation for learning, respect for evidence, and a classroom ethos that supports openness and sharing in learning.

Different kinds of motivation for undertaking learning activities have been identified and the importance of encouraging intrinsic motivation pointed out. This leads to learning with understanding, not the shallow learning that tends to follow when it is extrinsically motivated, that is, undertaken in order to gain the satisfaction of a reward, not for the satisfaction that the learning brings. Intrinsic motivation can be encouraged by

1. providing opportunity for children to interact with things in a way that encourages questioning and investigation. This means that

there should be plenty of materials available that are of interest to children at their particular stage.

2. giving the children some choice in their activity, even if this has to be limited choice, so that they acquire some ownership over it

3. involving the children in assessing their progress and solving the problems they encounter (see also Chapter 9)

4. setting up group work so that genuine collaboration is required to carry out the work

5. setting high expectations and showing confidence that all children can succeed

6. giving reasons for activities that have to be undertaken when children would rather be doing something else.

Some ways of encouraging children to realize that evidence is the basis for accepting scientific ideas are:

1. asking for evidence for children's claims and accepting whatever ideas fit the available evidence

2. avoiding the suggestion that the only worthwhile result is the "right" answer in terms of correct facts and conclusions

3. accepting what the children find from their investigation as the "right" answer, providing they have used their evidence and their reasoning

4. allowing children to make sense of their observations for themselves without imposing explanations that are outside their experience and comprehension

5. discussing how different evidence can affect the ideas that are accepted.

The teacher can encourage the classroom atmosphere that enables children to express their ideas without fear of being wrong and fosters the expression of curiosity and the desire to satisfy it by

1. appreciating children's efforts whatever their results may be

2. finding out about the children's attitudes and feelings through discussion and conversation with them and, importantly, listening to them

3. showing real interest in what they feel as well as what they think

4. using knowledge of their attitudes and feelings to set realistic expectations; not expecting more cooperation or responsibility than is appropriate to their maturity
5. providing a classroom organization that supports responsibility and enables them to achieve their best
6. encouraging effort and socially desirable behaviors, not just achievement
7. setting an example by being patient, sympathetic, encouraging, and fair.

Chapter 3

The Right Question at the Right Time

JOS ELSTGEEST

A child was reflecting sunlight onto the wall with a mirror. The teacher asked: "Why does the mirror reflect sunlight?" The child had no way of knowing, felt bad about it, and learned nothing. Had the teacher asked, "What do you get when you stand twice as far away from the wall?", the child would have responded by doing just that, and would have seen his answer reflected on the wall.

Another teacher took his class out to explore the surroundings. They came to a flower bed with what he called "four o'clock flowers." He asked: "Why do these flowers close in the early evening and open again in the morning?" Nobody, including the teacher, knew. The question came from the "testing reflex" that we all struggle with. He could have asked: "Would the same flower that closes at night open again the next morning?" And the children could have labeled some flowers and found out the answers.

I once witnessed a marvelous science lesson virtually go to ruins. It was a class of young secondary school girls who, for the first time, were let free to handle batteries, bulbs, and wires. They were busy incessantly, and there were cries of surprise and delight. Arguments were settled by "You see?", and problems were solved with, "Let's try!" Hardly a thinkable combination of batteries, bulbs, and wires was left untried. Then, in the midst of the hubbub, the teacher clapped her hands and, chalk poised at the blackboard, announced: "Now, girls, let us summarize what we have learned today. Emmy, what is a battery?" "Joyce, what is the positive terminal?" "Lucy, what is the correct way to close a circuit?" And the "correct" diagram was

25

deftly sketched and labeled, the "correct" symbols were added, and the "correct" definitions were scribbled down. And Emmy, Joyce, Lucy, and the others deflated audibly into silence and submission, obediently copying the diagram and the summary. What they had done seemed of no importance. The questions were in no way related to their work. The rich experience with the batteries and other equipment, which would have given them plenty to talk and think about and question, was in no way used to bring order and system into the information they actually did gather.

These teachers were asking the "wrong" questions, ones which were unproductive in encouraging the children's learning. But how does the teacher diagnose such a question?

What Is a "Wrong" Question?

Wrong questions tend to begin with such innocent interrogatives as *why, how,* or *what.* But this is deceptive, for many good questions, too, begin with similar expressions. The real character of wrong questions lies in their "wordiness." They are purely verbal questions which require wordy answers, often neatly dressed in bookish phrases. Generally the answers precede the questions and are to be found in textbooks. They can also be obtained from blackboards and preserved in copybooks. When, therefore, a wordy question is asked, children try to look for the words of the answer and are totally lost when they cannot be found. These questions are not problems to be solved. They draw away from scientific problem solving.

However, recognizing a "wrong" question is one thing, how to ascertain a "right" question is quite another. For what is a good question? A good question is the first step toward an answer; it is a problem to which there is a solution. A good question is a stimulating question, which is an invitation to a closer look, a new experiment, or a fresh exercise. The right question leads to where the answer can be found: to the real objects or events under study, there where the solution lies hidden. The right question asks children to show rather than to say the answer: they can go and make sure for themselves. I would like to call such questions "productive" questions, because they stimulate productive activity. There are productive questions of various sorts. In the course of a scientific study they usually follow a certain pattern, since the "answerability" of one type of question depends on experience obtained through endeavoring to answer questions of another kind.

Productive Questions

Attention-focusing questions

The simplest kind of productive question is the straightforward "have you seen" or "do you notice" type of question. These are sometimes indispensable, in order to fix attention on some significant detail which might easily be overlooked. Children frequently take care of these questions themselves by their constant exclamations of "Look here!", so the teacher need not always bother. Children ask these questions at all times but particularly at the introduction of new objects of study. The necessary initial exploration of new materials, the "messing about" and "getting to know you" stage of exploration, is very much a "can you see and do you notice" situation. The "what?" questions closely follow, of course. "What is it?" "What does it do?" "What does it show about itself?" "What happens?" "What do I find inside (outside)?" "What do I see, feel, hear?" And simple observation is the route to the first simple answers, followed by more complicated questions.

Measuring and counting questions

Questions such as "how many?", "how long?", and "how often?" are measuring and counting questions to which the children can check their answers themselves. They can use new skills, learn to use new instruments, and feel confident, for no teacher can challenge your measuring ruler. There are many situations in which these questions arise, and they lead naturally to the next category of questions: comparison questions. "Is it longer, stronger, heavier, more?" These are comparison questions and there are many ways of phrasing them. Often they are preceded by "how much?", which adds a quantitative aspect and necessitates greater accuracy.

27

Comparison questions

Other, more qualitative, comparison questions bring about sharper observation. For instance: "In how many ways are your seeds alike and how do they differ?" Things can differ in many respects, such as in shape, color, size, texture, structure, markings, and so forth. Carefully phrased comparison questions help children to bring order into chaos and unity in variety. Classifying, playing attribute games, making identification keys, or making tables of collected data are disguised comparison questions. These questions logically lead to another class of questions which make the children create a different situation, or environment, so they may expect to obtain a different result.

Action questions

These are the "what happens if" questions, which can always be truthfully answered. They entail simple experimentation and never fail to provide a result. They are productive questions of great value and particularly appropriate at the beginning of a scientific study to explore the properties of unfamiliar materials, of living or nonliving, of forces at work, and of small events taking place.

- What happens if you place your antlion in damp sand? What happens if you pinch the seed leaves off a young growing plant?
- What happens if you place a cutting or twig in water?
- What happens if you put your twig upside-down?
- What happens if you hold your magnet near a match?
- What happens if you throw a tiny piece of paper in a spider's web?

Innumerable good examples of "what happens if ..." problems can be given which lead to as many solutions that can be readily found to the satisfaction of the children and their teachers.

Working on "what happens if" problems, children are bound to discover some form of relationship between what they do and the reaction of the thing they handle. This greatly adds to the store of experiences that young children require. As adults, we often assume that children can fill in the generalizations and abstractions that we so casually throw around, but children must collect the "fillings" themselves. An exciting addition to solving "what happens if" problems is the challenge to predict the outcome. Initially the children will just guess, and find themselves way out in their predictions, but with the accumulation of experiences they become sharper. The ability to predict is a prerequisite to the ability to tackle real or, rather, more complicated problem-solving questions.

Problem-posing questions

After sufficient activities provoked by the type of questions just described, children become ready for a new type of question: the more sophisticated "can you find a way to" question. This will always set up a real problem-solving situation to which children enthusiastically respond, provided it makes sense to them.

I once asked a class of children, "Can you make your plant grow sideways?" For a short time they had been studying plants growing in tins, pots, boxes, and other contraptions made of plastic bags. I was just a little too anxious and too hasty and, quite rightly, I got the answer, "No, we can't." So we patiently continued with scores of "what happens if" experiments. Plants were placed in wet and dry conditions, in dark and in light corners, in big boxes and in cupboards, inside collars of white and black paper, upside down, on their side, and in various combinations of these. In other words, the children really made it "difficult and confusing" for the plants. Their plants, however, never failed to respond in one way or another, and slowly the children began to realize that there was a relationship between the plant and its environment, which they controlled. Noticing the ways in which the plants responded, the children became aware that they could somehow control the growth of plants in certain ways, because the responses of the plants became evident by the way they grew. Tips curved upwards, stems bent, plants grew tall and thin, or sometimes withered altogether. The children discovered that moisture, as well as light and position, affects the growth of plants.

When the question "Can you find a way to make your plant grow sideways?" reappeared later there was not only a confident reaction, there was also a good variety of attempts, all sensible, all based on newly acquired experience, and all original. Some children laid their plant on its side and rolled a newspaper tube around the container and the plant. Others manufactured a stand to hold a horizontal tube into

29

which they pushed the top of their plant (this one turned back). One group closed their plant inside a box with a hole, but they fixed a tube in the hole and directed it toward the light of the class window. Some just tied their plant sideways along a cross stick and added restricting strings as soon as the growing tip curled upward again.

It is obvious that "can you find a way to _____" questions must be preceded by a satisfactory exploration of the materials with which the children work. They need to investigate first what possibilities and impossibilities there are, and become familiar with some of the properties of the objects under study, particularly those properties which show up in interaction with (things out of) the environment. Source books and teacher's guides can never indicate when the children are ready for more formal, more complicated, problem solving. This is a matter to be decided either by the children themselves when they spontaneously begin to tackle such problems, or by the sound judgment of the teacher when he or she has sufficient evidence that the children can move on to more sophisticated activities. This is important to note, for if a teacher rigidly adheres to a (necessarily limited) outline in some textbook, there is a good chance that the children will get confused, and the class will end in chaos.

The "can you find a way to" question comes in many guises. "Can you make a mealworm turn around?" "Can you make a sinking object float?" "Can you separate salt from water?" It is in essence a prediction question, a more complicated "what happens if" question turned around. Finding the solution necessitates the forming of a simple hypothesis and consequent verification in a very direct manner. The acknowledgment of the need to recognize variables and to control them emerges naturally. This is the point where children's science begins to make real progress.

Teachers' How and Why Questions

Finally there follows a category of questions which we should approach with caution, as there is a serious danger of misusing them. They are what I call reasoning questions, and they often ask for some sort of explanation. Naturally these questions tend to start with *how* and *why*, and that is where the danger lies. The anxious teacher might want to let himself loose in worthy but wordy explanations which will not be rooted in the children's experience. Anxious children might easily mistake them for test questions to which, they often feel, they should have been given model answers. The lack of a model answer makes children afraid to be "wrong." But reasoning questions are very important in science education and we should never eliminate them. After all, every youngster is a born "how and why" questioner, so how could we avoid them? What we should eliminate, however, is the impression that to every question of this sort there is one right answer. Reasoning questions are not meant to be answered in a unique way. They are meant to make children think and reason independently about their own experiences. They are meant to make them reflect upon the relationships they have discovered or recognized, so they can carefully begin to draw conclusions, or make generalizations, on the strength of real evidence that they have collected or uncovered. These questions are intended to open up discussion, to make children freely express what and how they think about their observations and findings. The discussion, the dialogue, the sharing of ideas helps in recognizing new relationships and it aids understanding. It is essential that the children talk freely, that they are not held back by any red light of fear, for even the most preposterous statement can provoke argument, and argument leads to correction, provided it is based on found, and sound, evidence.

A child can more easily take responsibility for his answer if the question is presented with the little addition: "Why, do you think...?" In that case even though there may be something wrong with the thinking and the opinion may be subjected to fierce argument, the answer to the question will always be right. The child, after all, knows best what he thinks. (The same advice and more is given in Harlen 2000b.) Care is not only needed when phrasing these questions, but also in when they are presented. Children who are working with mosquito larvae for the first time may be effectively put off from further exploration and thought by a premature "Why do the larvae come to the surface of the water?" How would they know? They may have framed this question themselves, which is a sign that they do not know, so why ask them?

However, it may well happen that children have watched mosquito larvae wriggle down to the bottom, time after time, whenever they were disturbed by a waving hand, or by a knock on the jar that contained them, or by shaking or stirring the water in which they swam. These children would also see the larvae come up again and again; they might notice their tail tubes sticking up just above the surface of the water. They may time how long the larvae can stay under the water surface. Whenever the larvae come up, the children can discourage them from doing so by shaking the jar, or by knocking the sides of it. And what would the larvae do if you cover the surface of the water with snippets of paper or a sheet of cellophane? The children are bound to become aware of the larvae's persistence to reach the surface. Only after these and similar experiences can the children become involved in a sensible argument when asked, "Why do you think these larvae come up to the surface of the water?" In the first place, the "why" here is easily translated into "what for." Second, the children can now express their thoughts with confidence, because they have something to think and to talk about, all based on a series of common experiences to which they can refer. They can produce relevant evidence. Within the same frame of reference the teacher can now take part in the discussion as an equal. This is important, for the answer "They come up to breathe" is by no means an obvious one. Many water creatures never come up to breathe, and a tail is not readily associated with the act of breathing. Yet the teacher's contribution may point in the direction of respirational need without its becoming, for the children, an act of faith.

Children's How and Why Questions

There are a few more aspects of the "why" question which are useful to consider here. We cannot avoid the questions the children ask, and they often ask "Why?". The erroneous, though flattering, attitude of many parents and children tempts teachers often to bluff their way out with vague, exalted, impressive-sounding "answers," but this does not help the children. Of course, within their experience they can be given answers which point out relationships, but the experience is not always present. Breaking up the question into manageable "what happens if" questions and "let us see how" observations may try the children's patience, but will provide necessary experiences to make understanding possible. In any case, it is good science education.

Nevertheless, real difficulties can arise, for there are many "why" questions which simply have never been answered yet; others cannot even be answered by science. For instance, questions about why things are as they are lead us rapidly into the realm of metaphysics or theology or mythology. Worthy answers can be obtained, but these are to be found beyond science, and this should be made clear. But also within the bounds of human science there remain many questions yet unanswered, and even more to which the humble but honest teacher must admit, "I do not know." Well, it's best admit it, for this is a healthy lesson to the children. Science is the search for, rather than the answer to, our questions of why and how. Besides, both "why" and "how" are illusive questions. As soon as we approach a satisfying answer, we become aware of a new problem, and a fresh "why" or "how" shimmers above the horizon. We have not yet reached the final answer, to a single final "why?" or "how?", so the search continues, and it is into this search that we introduce our children. A great number of why questions are by nature queries of "what for?", "to what purpose?", or "where to?" and these refer to structure-function relationships. Other why questions search for cause-effect relationships, or ask why things behave the way they do. The teacher's attempt to break these questions up into simpler questions reveals their true nature, and the search for solutions begins to alternate between doing and reasoning.

The simple "becauses" reasoned out by the children themselves on the strength of their own evidence and their own experiences are far more valuable and important than any of the reasons provided by adults and faultlessly recited without understanding. Even an adult's understanding depends on his or her own step-by-step progress through masses of experiences, and many of us have understood things that we were supposed to have learned at school only years after we were set free to educate ourselves.

Teachers' Explanations

Children may be interested in solving problems that are beyond their scope, either because the necessary equipment is inadequate (or not refined enough) or because the required experimentation is simply too difficult or complicated. A knowledgeable teacher is then a great asset and can contribute considerably toward widening the children's horizon of learning and knowledge, because this teacher can fathom the depth of the children's ability and thus measure the quality and quantity of the information or explanation to be given. When children ask, they indicate that they want to know, and when they want to know, they are interested. Interest is a fertile ground in which the teacher's explanation is gratefully and fruitfully accepted. The clever teacher also recognizes that where questions arise and interest is present, functional literacy shows its worth. Children will be led to good books. Not only will they look for and find an answer to their problem, they will also find that other scientists have grappled with such a problem, and often they may appreciate how much effort and research was required in order to find a solution.

Summary of Main Points

This chapter has been concerned with one of the main forms of verbal communication between teacher and children: questioning and answering questions. The way in which a question is framed is a key factor in determining the effect it has since a question already has within it the kind of answer that can be given, even before it is spoken.

There are many different kinds of questions and their varying effect on children is striking. A distinction has been drawn between productive and unproductive questions according to whether or not they promote children's activity and reasoning. Questions that do *not* do this (unproductive questions) are those that ask only about knowledge of words, often for repetition of words given earlier by the teacher or to be found in a book. Questions which encourage activity (productive questions) come in various kinds and form a hierarchy reflecting the experience of the children.

Questions that promote reasoning often start with "why" or "how" and can be asked by teacher and children. It has been suggested that teachers' why questions should include the phrase "Why do you think," and should be carefully timed so that children have the necessary experience to form a view that is genuinely their own.

Children's why questions often present problems for a teacher, for not all can be answered and not all should be answered. Some ask about relationships that children can discuss; these can be turned into productive questions (see also Chapter 4).

The points emerging from this chapter lead to these suggestions for implementation:

Asking "productive" questions

1. Study the effect on children of asking different kinds of questions so that you can distinguish the "productive" from the "unproductive."
2. Use the simplest form of productive question (attention-focusing) during initial exploration to help children take note of details that they might overlook.
3. Use measuring and counting questions to nudge children from purely qualitative observation toward quantitative observation.
4. Use comparison questions to help children order their observations and data.
5. Use action questions to encourage experimentation and the investigation of relationships.
6. Use problem-posing questions when children are capable of setting up for themselves hypotheses and situations to test them.
7. Choose the type of question to suit the children's experience in relation to the particular subject of inquiry.

Suggestions for why and how questions

1. When asking questions to stimulate children's reasoning, make sure they include "what do you think about" or "why do you think."
2. Don't ask questions of this type until children have had the necessary experience they need so that they can reason from evidence.
3. When children ask why questions, consider whether they have the experience to understand the answer.
4. Don't be afraid to say you don't know an answer, or that no one knows (if it is a philosophical question).
5. Break up questions whose answers would be too complex into ones that concern relationships the children can find out about and understand.
6. Take children's questions seriously, as an expression of what interests them; even if the questions cannot be answered, don't discourage the asking.

Chapter 4

Helping Children Raise Questions— and Answering Them

SHEILA JELLY

In my experience, many of the questions children ask spontaneously are not profitable starting points for science. The commonest questions I get asked by five- to seven-year-olds are along the lines of, "Is Mr. Jelly your husband/father/brother?" I quote this not as a facetious example, but to make the point that questions from young children reflect an urge to make associations with their previous experience. Even when this associative process is triggered by interesting materials with great potential for scientific investigation, a child's curiosity often does not show itself as spontaneous questioning but rather as a statement of interests. "Look, it [a snail] has little eyes on stalks." In situations like this, teachers have to intervene in order to frame problems that children can investigate in a scientific way: "Are they really eyes?" "Can snails see?" "How might we find out?" So in practice it is very often a teacher's questioning, not a child's, that initiates scientific activity. For this reason any consideration of handling children's questions in science must be closely related to the way in which a teacher handles her own questioning.

In Chapter 3 a series of different types of questions was discussed. They were called productive because "they stimulate productive activity" and were distinguished from unproductive questions, which do not lead to scientific activity but the recall of factual knowledge. Unproductive questions are those to which a child either knows the answer ("Where did you find it?") or, if he does not ("What's it called?"), he obtains it from secondary sources—the teacher or books. Such questions may be very useful for encouraging conversation or, with the development of reading skills in mind, for sending children to books to acquire information, but as starting points for scientific activity they are very limited and unproductive. The features of these two types of question are summarized in the table below.

Unproductive	*Productive*
Promote science as information	Promote science as a way of working
Answers derived from secondary sources by talking/reading	Answers derived from firsthand experience involving practical action with materials
Tend to emphasize answering as the achievement of a correct end product (the right answer)	Encourage awareness that varied answers may each be "correct" in its own terms and view achievement as what is learned in the process of arriving at an answer
Successful answering is most readily achieved by verbally fluent children who have confidence and facility with words	Successful answering is achievable by all children

Productive questions are the type we need to encourage in the classroom if we wish to promote science as a way of working, but experience shows that teachers ask far more unproductive questions than productive ones, and they frequently find the framing of productive questions a difficult task. This is not at all surprising because most of us have acquired our formal education in bookish environments and have accordingly established questioning styles that tend to require factual answers. But it is important to make the effort to change the pattern of questioning, since productive questions are a very powerful tool for the teacher. They have considerable value when planning science work; they are extremely useful in those "thinking on the feet" situations where we make an instantaneous response to something a child says or does, and, importantly, they are the kind of questions that children can profitably "catch" if we wish them to find their own problems for investigation.

If we are to improve the range and quality of questioning in a classroom three things are required:

1. improve our own ability to ask questions
2. establish a climate of curiosity and questioning that is conducive to children's question asking
3. develop strategies for handling children's spontaneous questions.

Improving Teachers' Questioning Skills

From the various types of productive questions illustrated in Chapter 3 (see also Chapter 6), it is possible to see that there are general frameworks that can be applied in a variety of situations:

"Which _____ is best for _____ ?"

"Who has the _____ ?" (strongest hair, best sight, keenest hearing)

"Will it _____ if we _____ ?" (swing more quickly/make it longer)

"Do _____ prefer _____ ?" (any animal/any food or condition)

The key to generating specific questions for particular situations is practice. With this in mind, here are three activities for teachers to help improve questioning skills.

1. Try taping conversation when there is science work going on in the classroom. Later, analyze the questions the teacher asks. Are they unproductive or productive? What is the proportion of each type? Of the productive questions, what kind of child activity did each promote? This is a salutary experience for us all! The first analysis may well prove a little disheartening but, over time, it becomes very encouraging to note how questioning styles can alter.
2. Scrutinize the questions posed in primary science books. Are they unproductive or productive? If productive, what scientific experiences are they encouraging? Many teachers who have carried out this activity report an increased awareness of question types and an increased facility in generating their own productive questions.
3. Use odd moments to practice question finding. Suppose, for example, you are waiting in a parking lot (a useful situation, since all

schools will have one). What is its potential for science? What productive questions could you ask about it to stimulate children's scientific activity? Make a list of attention-focusing questions (see Chapter 3, page 27). Try to go beyond the obvious properties such as color/shape/size/kind/age and include questions involving patterns and relationships. For example:

> Which of the cars are rusting?
>
> Which parts of a car rust?
>
> Which parts have no rust?
>
> Do all cars rust in the same place?
>
> Is there any connection between the amount of rust and the age of a car?
>
> What attention-focusing questions might you ask about car tires, windows, or lights?

Try also to identify problem-posing questions (see Chapter 3, page 29), such as, "Which color for a car is the safest?" Can you think of other questions? What productive questions are appropriate for a study of the buildings around the car park?

It's also useful to apply question-finding practice to normal classroom events. Think, for example, of the water play area of a classroom for five- to seven-year-olds. The children will have observational experience of things that float and things that sink. How might their work be extended to involve fair-testing experience? What questions could they be asked? "Who can make the best boat?" is one that can promote interesting discussion and activity. Can you think of another?

Establishing a Classroom Climate Conducive to Children's Question Asking

If questioning styles are not taught, a teacher's verbal questioning will probably be the most important factor in establishing a climate conducive to question asking by children. But it is not the only factor, and so it is useful to consider ways by which curiosity might be aroused and how such curiosity can be linked to particular questioning frameworks. As a first step we need to get children's interest stimulated, and this means giving them direct contact with materials. It also means that we need to think carefully about the nature of the materials that make children curious. Materials the children bring in spontaneously have a built-in curiosity factor and need no further discussion; but what of materials selected by teachers? These can usefully be considered in two categories: those with immediate appeal, and those that are commonplace when seen through a child's eyes but that can evoke curiosity if teacher tactics present them in a new and challenging light. The first kind present the fewest problems because we know that certain properties such as color, shape, and movement can, in themselves, trigger curiosity. Indeed we constantly capitalize on these facts when we introduce materials into the classroom. But if we remember that children's response is shaped largely by what they guess to be the expectations their teacher has for them, then in many classes materials will promote activities of the kind summarized in Figure 4–1.

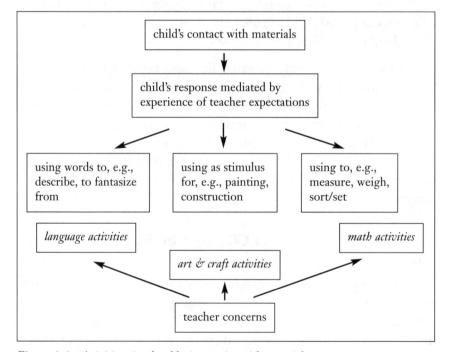

Figure 4–1. *Activities stimulated by interaction with materials*

Not surprisingly, therefore, a child's response tends to show itself as an application of the known (procedures and techniques), rather than in a concern for the unknown and an associated generation of questions. For this reason it is helpful to concentrate consciously on building up what we might call the questioning dimension in children's expectations of how the teacher would like them to respond. This dimension can be developed when they associate with a teacher's productive questioning style. It can also be strengthened by teacher-promoted activities that reinforce the style: activities that bring children into contact with materials linked to appropriate questions, and activities that provide opportunities for children to frame their own productive questions. Increased contact with appropriate questions can be achieved in a variety of ways. For example:

- by making sure that displays and collections have associated inquiry questions for the children to read, ponder, and perhaps explore incidentally to the main work of the class
- by introducing a problem corner or a "question of the week" activity where materials and associated questions are on offer to the children as a stimulus to thought and action that might be incorporated into classwork
- by making "questions to investigate" lists that can be linked to popular information books
- by ensuring that in any teacher-made science work cards or worksheets there is a question framed to encourage children to see their work as inquiry-based and also provides a useful heading for any resultant work displayed in the classroom

Opportunities for children to frame productive questions include activities such as:

- using regular class time (such as news time or equivalent) to encourage children to talk about something interesting they have observed, and to tell others of the questions it prompts
- encouraging children to supply "questions of the week" (as in the activity described above)
- establishing procedures by which children, having completed a piece of work, are encouraged to list further questions about it.

For example, individually when completing a work card or collectively when discussing work on display.

With techniques such as these it is often surprising how much the quality of children's questioning improves over a period of time. However, it should be stated that, initially, most children find this type of questioning a very difficult task and tend to ask only unproductive questions: They will need lots of encouragement. Quite clearly, too much emphasis on question asking too soon can be counterproductive and may result in a "not another question" dismissal rather than the excitement and enthusiasm we wish to develop.

Curiously, materials that are very "ordinary" in children's eyes often generate more sustained question asking than materials with obvious child appeal. Perhaps this is because a child's particular involvement with things with immediate appeal is sufficient satisfaction in itself, and further scrutiny becomes an intrusive and unwanted distraction. Whatever the reason, it is worth considering how commonplace things can be used to promote question-generating situations. For example:

- by using collections of everyday things as a focus for linking materials with teacher-framed questions. A collection of kitchen utensils, say, has little immediate appeal, but associated with appropriate questions it can provide challenging involvement. If, for example, the tools are sorted by function, many inquiry questions can follow. In time, children can be encouraged to organize their own collections of "ordinary" things and supply questions for others to investigate.
- by selecting materials for practical investigation that do unexpected things. As, for example, the effect of dropping a plasticine ball on polystyrene when investigating bouncing balls; anomalous happenings are very good question stimulators.
- by using magnifiers and microscopes to extend children's observation so that they will see exciting detail in familiar things.
- by considering the extent to which the conventional aesthetic approach to display can be broadened to include materials that may not be visually pleasing but that justify inclusion in display themes because of their potential for inquiry work. For example, a display

centered on the theme of the sea is made richer educationally by the inclusion of some tatty, ugly shoreline debris—if the material is linked to challenging questions.

Teacher tactics of the kind described undoubtedly improve the climate of inquiry in a classroom and, as a consequence, lead to more spontaneous questioning by children.

Handling Children's Spontaneous Questions

Spontaneous questions from children come in various forms and carry a variety of meanings. Consider for example the following questions. How would you respond to each?

1. What is a baby tiger called?
2. What makes it rain?
3. Why can you see yourself in a window?
4. Why is the hamster ill?
5. If I mix these paints, what color will I get?
6. If God made the world, who made God?
7. How long do cows live?
8. How does a computer work?
9. When will the tadpoles be frogs?
10. Are there people in outer space?

Clearly the nature of each question shapes our response to it. Even assuming we wanted to give children the correct answers, we could not do so in all cases. Question 6 has no answer, but we can of course respond to it. Question 10 is similar; it has no certain answer but we could provide a conjectural one based on some relevant evidence. All the other questions do have answers, but this does not mean that each answer is similar in kind, nor does it mean that all answers are known to the teacher, nor are all answers equally accessible to children.

When we analyze what we do every day as part of our stock-in-trade, namely respond to children's questions, we encounter a highly complex situation. Not only do questions vary in kind, requiring answers that differ in kind, but children also have different reasons for asking a question. The question may mean, "I want a direct answer," it might mean, "I've asked the question to show you I'm interested, but I'm not after a literal answer," or it could mean, "I've asked the question because I want your attention—the answer is not important." Given all these variables, how then should we handle the questions raised spontaneously in science work? The comment of one teacher is pertinent here:

> The children's questions worry me. I can deal with the child who just wants attention, but because I've no science background I take other questions at face value and get bothered when I don't know the answer. I don't mind saying I don't know, though I don't want to do it too often. I've tried the "let's find out together" approach, but it's not easy and can be very frustrating.

Many teachers will identify with these remarks, and what follows is a suggested strategy for those in a similar position. It's not the only strategy possible, nor is it completely fail-safe, but it has helped a large number of teachers deal with difficult questions. By "difficult questions" I mean those that require complex information and/or explanation for a full answer. The approach does not apply to simple informational questions such as 1, 7, and 9 on the last list because these are easy to handle, either by telling or by reference to books or expertise in ways familiar to the children in other subject areas. Nor is it relevant to spontaneous questions of the productive kind discussed earlier, because these can be answered by doing. Essentially it is a strategy for handling complex questions, and in particular those of the "why" kind that are the most frequent of all spontaneous questions. They are difficult questions because they carry an apparent request for a full explanation that the teacher may not know and that, in any case, is likely to be conceptually beyond a child's understanding.

The strategy recommended is one that "turns" the question to practical action with a "let's see what we can do to understand more" approach. The teaching skill involved is the ability to "turn" the question. Consider, for example, a situation in which children are exploring the properties of fabrics. They have dropped water on different types and become fascinated by the fact that water stays "like a little ball" on felt. They tilt the felt, rolling the ball around, and someone asks, "Why is it like a ball?". How might the question be turned by applying the "doing more to understand more" approach?

We need to analyze the situation quickly and use what I call a "variables scan." The explanation must relate to something "going on" between the water and the felt surface that causes the ball. That being so, ideas for children's activities will come if we consider ways in which the situation could be varied to better understand the making of the ball. We could explore surfaces, keeping the drop the same, and explore drops, keeping the surface the same. These thoughts can prompt others that bring ideas nearer to what children might do. For example:

1. Focusing on the surface, keeping the drop the same:

    What is special about the felt that helps make the ball? Which fabrics are good "ball-makers"?

    Which fabrics are poor?

    What do the good ball-making fabrics have in common? What surfaces are good ball-makers?

    What properties do these surfaces share with the good ball-making fabrics?

    Can we turn the felt into a poor ball-maker?

2. Focusing on the water drop, keeping the surface the same:

    Are all fluids good ball-makers?

    Can we turn the water into a poor ball-maker?

Notice how the "variables scan" results in the development of productive questions that the children can explore. The original question has been turned to practical activity and children exploring along these lines will certainly enlarge their understanding of what is involved in the phenomenon. They will not arrive at a detailed explanation but may be led toward a simple generalization of their experience, such as "A ball will form when . . ." or "It will not form when . . . ."

Some teachers see the strategy as one of diversion (which it is) and are uneasy that the original question remains unanswered, but does this matter? The question has promoted worthwhile scientific inquiry, and we must remember that its meaning for the child may well have been "I'm asking to communicate my interest." For such children interest has certainly been developed, and children who may actually have initiated the question as a request for explanation are normally satisfied by the work their question generates.

The strategy can be summarized as follows:

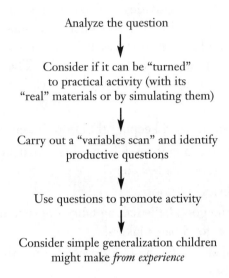

Analyze the question

Consider if it can be "turned"
to practical activity (with its
"real" materials or by simulating them)

Carry out a "variables scan" and identify
productive questions

Use questions to promote activity

Consider simple generalization children
might make *from experience*

This strategy is not a blueprint for handling all difficult questions, but it does provide a framework that helps us to cope with many of them. Its use becomes easier with practice. Try using it to respond to Question 3 on page 43 (a comparatively simple application) and to the question "Why do airplanes stay up?", which is a more complex application. The task may be difficult initially; indeed, several aspects of the analysis and use of questions put forward in this chapter may prove likewise. But the effective handling of questions is vital in any science program.

Summary of Main Points

Children learn their question-asking habits from teachers. If children are to be encouraged to raise questions that lead to investigation, this is one more reason (added to those given in Chapter 3) for teachers to make the effort to ask more productive questions and fewer unproductive ones. Some specific ways in which teachers can practise and improve question skills are:

1. Provide a wide range of materials for children to respond to.
2. Practise and improve your questioning style so that it provides an example for the children.
3. Provide a climate of inquiry for children to work in.
4. Encourage children to form and to discuss their own questions.
5. Respond positively to children's spontaneous questions.
6. Turn children's unproductive questions into productive ones that promote investigation of real materials.

The atmosphere in the classroom must also be conducive to encouraging children to ask questions. Some ways of showing that questions are welcome are by adding questions to displays and collections, introducing a problem corner in the classroom, creating lists of "questions to investigate," and making sure any work cards or worksheets are framed in terms of investigable questions. Regular discussion of questions is also important. Children, like teachers, do not find it easy at first to change the emphasis in their questioning from unproductive to productive. Novel materials are not necessarily the best stimulus; often more familiar ones help children raise questions, especially with a lead from the teacher to the kind of productive questions that can be asked.

Once children begin to ask questions they will ask ones of all kinds; some will be difficult for teachers to handle, but it is important to find a way of doing so that does not make the child wish he or she had not asked. A strategy has been described for analyzing children's questions so that unproductive ones can be used productively.

Chapter 5

Taking Children's Own Ideas Seriously

*T*his chapter is about using and developing children's own ideas. To do this means taking their ideas seriously. We are concerned here with the reasons for doing this, but more importantly with how teachers can find out what ideas children hold and with what they can do to use these ideas as the starting point for working toward more scientific ideas. To illustrate the meaning of taking children's ideas seriously, or not, Roger Osborne, in Chapter 7 of the first edition of this book, related this classroom observation:

> I recently spent the day with a class of nine-year-old children and their teacher. During the course of the day the children had a lesson on foods and taste. The teacher was well prepared in that she had undertaken some background reading on the subject and had prepared an activity which would involve children tasting various foods. To begin the lesson the teacher asked the class, "Why do we eat food?" Thirty eager hands leapt skywards. Answers seriously offered included, "to help us come alive in the morning (breakfast)," "to stop us feeling hungry," "so that we don't get tired." It soon became apparent that while these ideas were listened to by the teacher, they were not the one or ones that she wanted. Each answer in turn received a cursory nod of acceptance from the teacher but was passed over apparently in search of an answer which the teacher considered to be more scientifically acceptable.

This way of paying lip service to children's ideas, but not really attending to them, is still very common. This is despite the fact that, in the two decades since these observations were made, much has been found out and written about the importance of not ignoring students' responses, as this teacher was in effect doing. Roger Osborne and his team in New Zealand were among the first to research the ideas that students bring to their science lessons (e.g., Freyberg, Osborne, and Tasker 1983). These researchers, and other teams in the U.S. and the U.K., began by studying the ideas of secondary school students and later moved to look at what was happening at earlier stages.

Years before, Piaget had alerted us to the fact that children are working things out for themselves right from birth, and often arrive at what we call "nonscientific" ideas. For example, if you pour water from a tall narrow container into a wide one, the quantity does look to have changed, so if you judge only from appearances, then you would conclude that the amounts were different. Piaget showed that young children often form their ideas from appearances rather than from logical argument about whether anything has been added or taken away. However, while Piaget helped us to become aware of the ideas that children hold, it was much later that the implications for education were addressed. The reasons for taking children's ideas seriously become clear if we look at some examples. In the first part of this chapter, we present a selection of children's ideas about a few science concepts—living things, simple circuits, light, sound, and floating and sinking—from the wide range that have been investigated in recent years. Then we consider what a teacher can do to help children to change their ideas and develop more scientific ones.

Examples of Children's Ideas

Children's ideas about living things

An investigation of children's meanings for the word "animal" was carried out by Beverly Bell in New Zealand (Bell 1981). She showed children pictures of various living things including a cow, a person, a whale, a spider, and a worm. For each picture the child was asked, "In your meaning of the word animal, do you consider this to be an animal?" Irrespective of whether the answer was yes or no, the child was asked to give the reasoning that had led to the response. "Why do you think that?" and "Can you tell me your reasons?" were typical questions asked by the interviewer. Interviews established that many children consider animals to be only the larger land mammals, such as those found on a farm, in a zoo or jungle, or in the home as pets. The reasons used by many children to categorize something as an animal included the number of legs (animals have four), the size (they are big), the habitat (they live on land) and the skin covering (animals have fur). Surveys were designed to establish what percentage of children at various age levels consider a cow, a person, a whale, a spider, and a worm to be an animal. Typical results are shown in Figure 5–1. The sixteen- and seventeen-year-olds were studying biology; all other children were studying general science.

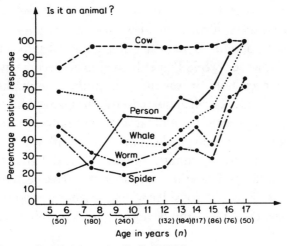

Figure 5–1. *Do you think it is an animal? (Bell 1981)*

The same researcher also found that children often use the word *plant* in a restricted way. Bell interviewed ten-year-olds, thirteen-year-olds and fifteen-year-olds and found children at all these ages who considered a tree not a plant. A ten-year-old told her, "No, it was a plant when it was little, but when it grows up it wasn't, when it became a tree it wasn't." Almost half the children interviewed considered that a carrot and a cabbage were not plants; they were vegetables. Over half did not consider a seed to be plant material even at the age of fifteen following considerable exposure to science (Osborne and Freyberg 1985, 7).

Children also have ideas about things that they can't see for themselves, such as the inside of an incubating egg, or the bones in their own bodies. For example, the drawings in Figure 5–2 were produced

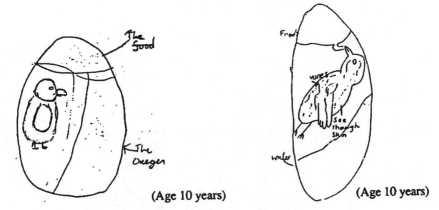

Figure 5–2. *What do you think is inside the egg? (SPACE Research Reports Growth 1990)*

by some children when their teacher borrowed an incubator and some fertile hen's eggs. Clearly all the children knew that a chicken would emerge and was forming somehow. Their teacher asked them to draw what they thought was inside the incubating eggs, to which they responded with a variety of ideas, some indicating development but most just growth of a perfectly formed tiny chick to a larger one.

Ideas about electric current

Work that involved interviewing children in the U.K., U.S., and New Zealand suggested that elementary school children have ideas about how electric current flows in a simple circuit. Children have been found to hold four different views, described in Figure 5–3 (Osborne 1983). The majority of primary children given a battery, bulb, and wires attempt to light the bulb by connecting the top terminal of the battery to the base of the bulb. Even when these children are shown that a second wire is necessary, some of them still retain a Model A view of current flow: "The current goes from the battery to the bulb where it is all used up." These children sometimes consider the non-current-carrying wire to be "a sort of switch" (initiates current flow) or a kind of safety wire. Model B is a very popular model among primary children: "The currents clash in the bulb causing it to light up." Model C is a view held more frequently by older children. These children seem to appreciate the circulatory nature of current but they

Electric current causes a light bulb to glow

A battery is connected up to a torch bulb as shown in the diagram. The bulb is glowing

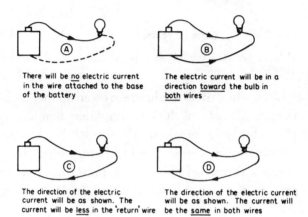

In the way you think about it, the <u>electric current</u> in the wires is best described by which diagram ?

(A) There will be <u>no</u> electric current in the wire attached to the base of the battery

(B) The electric current will be in a direction <u>toward</u> the bulb in <u>both</u> wires

(C) The direction of the electric current will be as shown. The current will be <u>less</u> in the 'return' wire

(D) The direction of the electric current will be as shown. The current will be the <u>same</u> in both wires

Figure 5–3. *What do you think is happening in the circuit? (Osborne 1983)*

consider that "some current must be used up to make the bulb glow." Finally, Model D is the accepted scientific view. While even some nine-year-olds hold this view, it is not the most popular view. Young children, when asked what they think of Model D, tend to reject it. "How could the bulb light or the battery go flat?" they ask.

Ideas about light

Investigations of children's ideas about light have shown remarkable similarity in relation to the role of the eye in seeing things. Children who are past the stage of believing that objects no longer exist if they are hidden from view or if they close their eyes, nevertheless describe the process of seeing as if it is their eyes that produce the light that makes the objects appear. Figure 5–4 shows a ten-year-old's drawing of how you see a light from a candle.

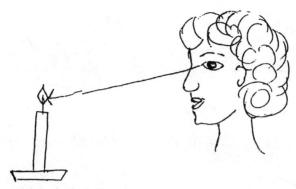

Figure 5–4. *The "active eye" indicated in a ten-year-old's drawing (SPACE Research Reports Light 1990)*

It is perhaps understandable that the eye is seen as an active agent rather than a receiver, for this fits the subjective experience of "looking." When we choose to look at something, we do feel our eyes turn as if we are the active agent in the process, and indeed the arrow from receiver to object does represent the line of sight. You would think that this idea could easily be challenged by the fact that we can't see in the dark. However, children have an answer to this:

> With no light your eyes cannot see anything as soon as you turn the light on your eyes can see again your eyes sort of work like a light when there's no light you can't see but when there is light you can see. (Harlen 2000a, 51)

Ideas about sound

Children more readily form ideas about the ear's role as a receiver in hearing sound than they form equivalent ideas about the eye. This may be because the sources of sounds are more obvious than the sources of light, which enable objects to be seen by reflecting rather than emitting light. In research carried out in the U.K. by the SPACE project, children's ideas about sound were explored after they had opportunity to make sound with a variety of instruments.

The simplest mechanism suggested for a drum's making a sound is that the impact of hitting produces "sound." However in Figure 5–5 a student explains the sound in terms of vibration. But notice that the vibration comes out of the drum through "the holes." A very common

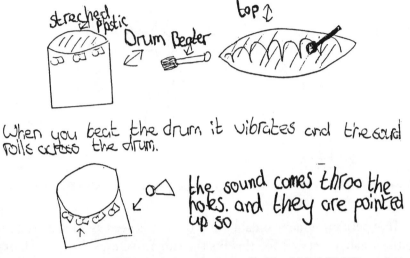

Figure 5–5. *How do you think the drum makes a sound? (Unpublished SPACE research)*

understanding of children is that sound travels through air, or at least through holes in solid objects and not through the solid itself.

The notion of "vibration" is associated with sound in ambiguous ways, sometimes sound being the same as vibration and sometimes having some cause-and-effect relationship to it. Often vibrations are linked with the source when they are directly observable but not otherwise. The explanation a ten-year-old gave to accompany a drawing of a "string telephone" made with yogurt cups and string illustrates the struggle to connect the two (Figure 5–6).

Ideas about floating and sinking

Floating is a phenomenon depending on the balance of forces acting on an object in water, but children often consider that other factors are involved, such as the speed of movement of the object and the depth of the water. In addition the concept of what is "floating" is problematic. Some research in New Zealand (Biddulph and Osborne 1984) explored what children understood *floating* to mean by using cards showing pictures of various objects in water, some floating and some not. When discussing the pictures showing objects floating with part above the water surface and part below (a person floating in a life-jacket, for instance), the children's decision as to whether or not

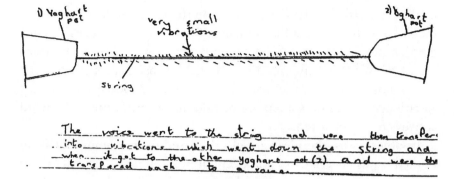

Figure 5–6. *How do you think a string telephone works?* (*Unpublished SPACE research*)
The voices went to the string and were then transfered into vibrations which went
down the string and when it got to the other yoghart pot and were then transfered
back into a voice.

it was floating appeared to be influenced by how much of the object
was above the water and how much below the surface. If a large proportion was above the surface there was general agreement that it was
floating, but if only a small part was above the surface (as in the case
of a bottle floating with only the neck above water) there were many
who said it was partly floating and partly sinking. A nine-year-old was
reported as saying in an interview that "It's floating and not floating.
The top is floating and the bottom's not."

The inferred movement of an object also affected judgment as to
whether or not it was floating. Young children claimed that the speed-
boat shown in a picture in a way that clearly indicated movement was
not floating because it was moving. An eight-year-old said, "It's going
fast, and floating is staying still and floating around." With objects
totally submerged (such as a person snorkeling), just under a half
described them as not floating.

Why Might Children Hold These Ideas?

Some reasons for the ideas children hold are not difficult to realize.
For example, as Osborne and others have pointed out, signs in shops
such as "No animals allowed" would reinforce a narrow view of the
notion of animal. So would the label "animal house" in a zoo and the
distinction between animals and fish that tends to be part of the
common usage of the words. These everyday ways of using the word

conflict with the "correct" use, based on the common features shared by all animals. The conflict can have serious consequences in children's misunderstanding if there is any uncertainty as to which meaning of the word is being used in a particular instance. A teacher can do nothing to prevent the word from being used loosely in everyday situations but can do something to find out what meaning the word conveys to the children.

In other cases, the ideas are clearly based on reasoning but from limited experience. For example, children often consider that rust is something that comes from within a metal, rather than something that forms on the outside. This is quite reasonable if they have only seen rust under flaking paint work or on the outside of nails, where it often looks, as one child wrote, as if it is "something that leaks out of a nail" (Association for Science Education 1998b).

Children also focus on one thing as a cause for a particular effect, rather than taking into account the possibility of other factors being important. For example, children aged six or seven might say that plants need water or light or soil to grow, but not all of these. They are also deceived by appearances, as we noted earlier; if the amount of water looks to be different after being poured from one container to another, then it is different.

These points suggest that there is some thinking behind the children's ideas. This may not be reasoning that will match up to scientific reasoning, but nonetheless it has produced ideas that the children have worked out for themselves and that make sense to them at that time. And for all of us, the ideas we have worked out are the ones that we believe. Indeed, there is plenty of research evidence that children will continue to believe their own ideas even when taught the "correct" scientific view (which they may learn by rote for the sake of passing tests, but don't really believe or understand). The current in a simple circuit is a case in point. Students in high school may be able to recall and manipulate Ohm's law but still believe that there is more current in the wire going toward a bulb than in the one leading away from it.

So we see that the children's ideas do not arise from imagination or fantasies, but are the product of their thinking. These ideas are often not consistent with scientific concepts and will not serve to help understanding as experience extends. Moreover, they often result from immature thinking processes, where only partial evidence has been gathered and taken into account, and like has not been compared with like. So if children are to advance their understanding of the world around them they have to develop ideas that are more widely useful, that is, scientific. It is evident, though, that the starting point has to be their ideas, not the scientific ones. The first step, then, is to find out what these ideas are.

Finding Out Children's Ideas

The first and most important point to make is that the classroom ethos has to be one in which the children feel free and comfortable to express their own ideas and ways of thinking, without fear that they will be giving the "wrong" answers (see Chapter 2). Given such a supporting climate, there are several ways in which teachers can gain access to children's thinking. The main ones are questioning, using children's drawings and concept maps, discussion (sometimes stimulated by introducing problems, as in a "concept cartoon," see Figure 5–8 on page 59) and, of course, listening.

Asking children questions at the start of a lesson or topic is a favorite way for teachers to try to link into children's thinking, as we saw with the teacher described at the start of this chapter. But the form of question needs thought. It should invite more than a one-word answer and encourage children to say what they really think. This chapter's opening situation would have been more productive if the teacher had said "Why *do you think* we eat food?" The simple reference to "what do you think" is highly significant here. A question such as "What difference do you think it will make if the water is stirred?" is preferable to "Will the salt dissolve more quickly if the water is stirred?"

The most useful questions for accessing children's ideas are the ones described as "open" and "person-centered." Person-centered questions are phrased to ask directly for the children's ideas, not the "right" answer. So, a question such as "Why do you think the cress grows better in this soil" is preferable to "Why does the cress grow better in this soil?" (See also Chapter 3 on phrasing questions for different purposes.)

Questions phrased in the same way can be used to ask children to make drawings—"draw what you think is happening inside the egg" was the stimulus to the drawings on page 51, for example. If the teacher is interested in children's ideas about change, then students might be asked to make a series of drawings such as a "comic strip" showing, for example, what the material of their T-shirt was like before it was a T-shirt, what that material came from, and so on.

Other useful drawings are *concept maps*. (See Figure 5–7.) Concept mapping has various meanings. In this context it refers to making links between concepts. As such it is a very direct way of gaining access to children's ideas, but it needs to be carefully tailored to particular children to ensure that they are familiar with the words that are used. The approach is to represent links between words by means of labeled arrows indicating the direction and nature of the relationship. When several concepts are linked together, the relationships form a web or map. The process is very easy even for the youngest children to grasp and the product gives some insight into the way they associate things together or see cause and effect. In some cases, particularly for young children, it helps to have the words written on cards so that they can be moved around. Arrows also on cards can be laid between words the children want to join. It is important for the linking words to be written, either by the child, or by the teacher for the child, because it is the nature of the link that gives the clue to the way the child is making sense of the things. These maps can be used before and after activities to see how ideas have or have not changed.

All of these strategies are helped by discussion with the teacher, so that the meaning of drawings and the words children are using can be clarified. It also helps to set up situations where children have group discussions. They might be explaining something that they have investigated, or discussing a new situation such as might be presented in a "concept cartoon" (see Figure 5–8) and debating alternative explanations. The teacher then just listens in on the conversations, picking up the words and ideas that the students are using.

Listening is a key activity for teachers who want to find out children's ideas. Children pick up and use words (often from the teacher) without a full grasp of their meaning. This was illustrated in the case of "vibration" and "floating"; other common examples are "evaporation," "dissolving," and "reflection." It is equally common to find young children, particularly boys, talking about black holes, electrons,

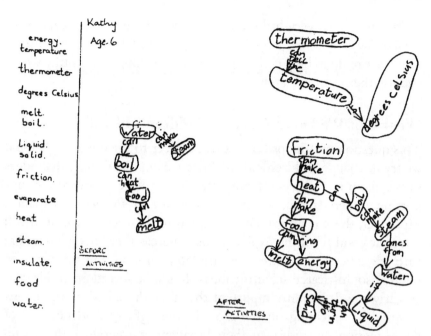

Figure 5–7. *A six-year-old's concept map (reproduced from Harlen et al. 1990, 13.7)*

Figure 5–8. *A concept cartoon (from Naylor and Keogh 2000)*

and protons with very little notion of what these words mean—they display the words like trophies. Below and in Chapter 8 we discuss what we can do to help children grasp the meaning of scientific words and use them appropriately.

What Can We Do to Change Children's Ideas?

This question presupposes a positive answer to the question "should we try to change children's ideas?" Even though children's own ideas satisfy them at the present time, they will not be adequate for supporting understanding as their experience of the world expands. Moreover, there is no evidence that, left to themselves, children will arrive at good scientific explanations, whereas there *is* evidence that early ideas persist and interfere with later learning. But this is not to say that sophisticated scientific ideas should be forced on children at an early age. It is more important that they should adopt the habits of mind of reflecting on the ideas in the light of evidence and of reconsidering their ideas as their broadening experience throws up new evidence. In this way understanding will be progressive, and ideas, as we said in Chapter 1 (page 8), will be "subjected to critical examination, and modified and reconstructed, if necessary, in the light of evidence."

So what can teachers do to facilitate this development and ensure that ideas become progressively more scientific? It isn't possible to be definite about this in any particular case because, until the ideas are revealed, the teacher will not know exactly what will be needed. But although we can't be prescriptive about when to use a particular approach, the teacher can be prepared to select from a range of strategies that recent research and experience have shown to be effective. The strategies can be matched to the likely reason for the children's nonscientific ideas. We saw that children's ideas may not be scientific for several reasons: they may be formed from limited experience, be influenced by perceptions rather than logic, take account of only one of several relevant features, result from faulty reasoning or use of nonscientific process skills, be specific to one context, and indicate a misunderstanding of words. In each case the possible reason points to the strategy that teachers might use in response, as suggested in Figure 5–9.

Basis of children's idea	*Response*
Limited experience	Provide wider experience that challenges the idea—e.g., plants growing without soil, wood that doesn't float, hearing sound through water and solid material
Based on perception rather than logic	Investigate further, focus on the process of change not just on the starting and ending conditions, leading to a different interpretation of the perception
Focused on one feature, ignoring others	Ask them to go on thinking: "Anything else?" "Would it be enough just to give the plant water?"
Faulty reasoning	Help children to test their ideas more rigorously (fairly) and to use all the evidence in drawing a conclusion
Tied to a particular context	Encourage them to apply the idea in a different but related context to see if it still "works"—"Can the idea that water vapor condenses from the air explain the moisture on cold cans taken out of the fridge?"
Misunderstanding of words	Ask them for examples of what they mean and introduce scientific terms alongside the ones children use—e.g., "see-through" or "transparent"

Figure 5–9. *Matching the response to children's ideas*

Most important, however, is to help children realize that there are different ideas from their own and to help them treat all ideas—their own and others'—as worthwhile only if there is supporting evidence. In many cases the response requires the introduction of alternative ideas from the ones the children have formed. Also, nonscientific ideas often persist despite contrary evidence simply because there is no better alternative way of explaining that is available to the children. Teachers are often unclear about how, when, or whether to introduce the scientific view of things. They often fear that the children will not understand and will be more confused, or that the teachers themselves will not be able to explain it in ways that the children can understand. Consequently, children may be left with their own "everyday" way of thinking when in fact they could be trying out ideas that expand their understanding. There are two important points to make here. One is that the teacher, although an important source, is not the only one who can contribute alternative ideas. Others are

- other children
- books, films, videos, CD-ROMs, the Internet
- other adults
- visits and fieldwork outside the classroom

The second important point is that the teacher has a role as an interface between the children and new ideas, whatever their source. A key feature of this role is to "scaffold" new ideas: that is, to introduce them at a time and in a way that helps children to advance their ideas towards the scientific view. The teacher's role in scaffolding is to support children in using an idea that they have not yet made "their own." A good example of this is shown in Figure 5–10, where the teacher of seven- and eight-year-olds used a soccer ball to help children develop their understanding of light being reflected. The children did not make the link for themselves, but were able to learn from it and transferred the idea to a mirror, using the hole in unifix cubes to identify their line of sight. Elsewhere I compared scaffolding to children trying on new clothes (Harlen 2000a). The analogy is quite apt, since new clothes for growing children are always chosen to be just a little larger, but not too much.

Involving the Children

Since it is the children who do the learning—no matter how much help is given, no one can do it for them—the more the children are "in the know" about what they are striving toward and how they can judge their own progress, the better. Teachers can share with children the goals of their learning in a variety of ways (see Chapter 9). They can also help children to realize how their ideas have changed and what brought about the change. Taking children into the discussion

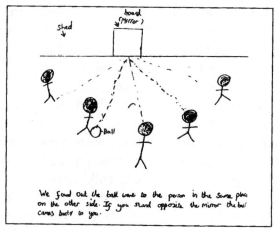

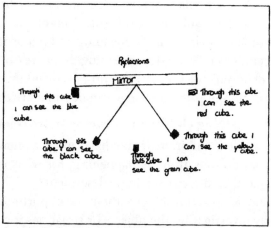

Figure 5–10. *Scaffolding an idea about reflection of light (ASE 1998b)*

of what and why they are learning will help them to become self-regulated and lifelong learners. Then we will have a more elaborated view of what it means to "take children's ideas seriously." It means not only taking seriously their ideas about what they are learning but also doing the same for their ideas about their learning processes.

Summary of Main Points

Children come to science activities with their own ideas about the things that are studied, rather than with empty spaces in their minds ready to be filled with new ideas. Their existing ideas are likely to be rather different from the accepted "scientific" ones and will strongly influence the sense children make of the activities they undertake. Unless teachers take particular care to find out about children's existing ideas and take deliberate steps to help children rethink their ideas and try out new ones as well as their own, these nonscientific ideas tend to persist and keep out the accepted scientific ones.

This chapter has given some examples from research into children's ideas about living things, electric circuits, light, sound, and floating and sinking. Some possible reasons why children hold these ideas have been discussed. These include reasoning that is based on limited experience, is influenced by perception, ignores some relevant features, may be specific to a particular context, or result from faulty reasoning. They can also be the result of a problem of communication, when teachers use words in their scientific meaning and pupils take them as having a different, often "everyday" meaning. Some reasons for wanting to change children's ideas have been proposed and the suggestions made for ways of bringing about change can be summarized as follows:

Suggestions for helping children to develop more scientific ideas

1. Find out what ideas children already have about a phenomenon or situation; what do they think is happening, for what reasons, and what words do they use to explain or describe it?
2. Take children's ideas seriously; give them the opportunity to try out their ideas by investigating the objects or situations for themselves.
3. Challenge children in discussion to find evidence for their own ideas.
4. Organize whole-class discussions so that different ideas about the same things can be brought together.
5. Enable children to become aware of and to try out ideas different from their own.
6. Offer them a scientific view as one worth trying as well as others; don't insist that it is "right" but let children explore its value for themselves.
7. Provide challenges for them to use new or modified ideas in trying to solve other problems or to make sense of a new experience and then to review their previous ideas and become aware of the change.

Chapter 6

Helping Children to Plan and Interpret Investigations

Investigation is a word implying different kinds of activity in different contexts. Detectives investigate crimes; historians investigate events long past; scientists investigate the effects of changes they observe or create; children investigate the things they find around them. What is the same about these is that they all involve observation or study by close examination and systematic inquiry (Webster's Collegiate Dictionary, 10th ed.). In the context of children learning science we associate investigation with practical, hands-on activity, but it is important to recognize that some investigations may not involve actual manipulation of objects but instead use evidence from secondary sources. For instance, information now available in visual and readily accessible forms on CD-ROMs and from the Internet can enable children to investigate questions and test their ideas. A good example is a class of nine-year-olds who used such sources to answer their question about why some animals have eyes at the front of their head and other have eyes at the sides. However, all investigations involve collecting and using evidence; that is, "minds-on" activity.

Different Kinds of Investigations

In this chapter we are primarily concerned with practical, firsthand investigations by children. But these are not all of the same kind, and it is important to recognize the differences and ensure that children have experience of all kinds, since these emphasize different process skills. These different types of investigation answer different questions. As described in Chapter 3, the main question types are

"I wonder what happens when _____ ?" questions seek and use information about things without changing them.

"I wonder what happens if _____ ?" questions seek and use information about what happens if you do change something.

"I wonder whether _____ ?" questions seek and use information to identify relationships and patterns.

"I wonder how we can _____ ?" questions seek to solve problems.

Information-seeking investigations

These are inquiries where children find out, mainly by observing what happens, for example, when eggs hatch, when water freezes, when colored ice is put into clear water and vice versa, when silkworms spin their cocoons, when spiders weave their webs. Very often they concern natural events, where there is no attempt to change things or make comparisons. They extend children's experience and are relevant at all stages in the primary school, but particularly for the very young children. For older children they will probably be the first step toward some other kind of investigation. These require little planning by the children—just some attention-focusing questions from the teacher.

Action-testing investigations

These involve children doing something to change the situation being investigated. This might be very simple, such as putting seeds in damp cotton wool to see if they germinate, sprinkling water on wild oat seeds, holding a magnet near a candle flame, and similar events suggested by the action questions on page 28 in Chapter 3. Or they may be more complex, such as comparing the effect on different materials when the same thing is done to them to test their strength, water absorbency, fire resistance, or other properties. In all these cases it is necessary to take steps to be sure that the effects observed are actually the result of the change made and not the result of something else, or not something that would have happened anyway. There is, therefore, much more to do in planning and interpreting these kinds of investigation and we shall discuss this later.

Pattern-finding investigations

These can be an extension of either of the first two types of investigation. For example, information-seeking questions can give rise to looking for patterns in natural events, such as in the weather ("red sky at night, shepherd's delight, red sky in the morning, shepherd's warning") and action-testing questions can lead to seeking patterns in, for instance, the notes produced by blowing across the top of bottles with different amounts of water in them, or how far a toy truck will travel after rolling down a slope held at different angles. In these investigations there is a greater emphasis on the interpretation of findings and checking whether the pattern identified is really supported by the evidence. The interpretation may involve considering the meaning of any relationship that is found between two variables. This is not necessarily one of direct cause and effect. For instance, when a clockwork toy car is found to move further the greater the number of turns of the key, the direct cause is not the key but the energy put into the spring by turning it.

How-to-do-it investigations

These are problems where the end product is given and the investigation concerns how to reach it. They are on the border between science and technology. Often the problem is to construct something—a bridge that will support a certain load, or a tower of a certain height. In other cases it is to make something happen—as in the example of making a plant grow sideways (page 29), or a pendulum that swings exactly once per second. They require application of scientific ideas about how materials or forces or living things behave. For that reason they have to build upon experience of investigations of other types.

Planning Investigations

We now turn to how to help children to develop their ability to plan investigations and to interpret what they find. Only when they do these things in a scientific manner will their observation and inquiry lead to the development of scientific ideas that help their understanding of things around. First we consider what is involved in planning if relevant and reliable evidence is to be obtained. Later we discuss the interpretation of the evidence obtained. So what should a plan include?

Here are some plans written by some ten- to eleven-year-olds. During a lesson about growth, the group was discussing which parts of their bodies grow most quickly, and their teacher asked them to write down what test they would do to find out if their fingernails grew faster than their toenails. These quotations are the complete answers of the children concerned, with the original spelling and punctuation preserved.

BRIAN: To describe it I would cut my nails right down and see which ones would grow first the quickest thats how I would do it.

LISA: You could keep checking your finger nails and toe nails for a week and keep all your infamation on a block chart then at the end of the week you can see which grows faster.

LEROY: My test would be I would cut my finger nails and I would cut my toe nails and in a week or two I would see how long they have grown and if my toe nails are longer they grow faster.

JOHN: I would measure them each day to see which had grown faster.

CANDY: At the begining of a 2 week period I would measure the length of my toe nails and I would also measure the length of my finger nails. At the end of the 2 weeks I would measure them both again and I would then know if my toe nails grow faster than my finger nails by taking the measurement of the beging of the two weeks from the measurement at the end of the two weeks.

As these were written plans they are undoubtedly limited by the children's ability to express themselves on paper, and we are probably right in supposing that the children could explain what they mean much more precisely in discussion. However, if we take these at face value for the moment, and don't read into them what is not there, it is interesting to see to what extent each contains the important elements of a plan.

At first reading it seems that the general approach of all five children is fairly sound. They all perceive the problem as one of comparing rates of growth. Measurement seems to be implied, but in fact only John and Candy actually mention measuring something. Brian has not identified what is to be measured at all and has done scarcely more than change "find out which grows faster" into "see which ones would grow . . . the quickest." Of course, he may know how "quickest" would be measured in practice, but we can't tell from what he has written.

Lisa says she would "keep checking" the nails for a week but does not state that she would "check" them both at the same time, which would be important for the sort of comparison she has in mind. Lisa and John state that they would be looking for changes from day to day (Brian indicates no time period) although their experience might well have taught them that little measurable change would have taken place in one day. However, by regular measurement they avoid Leroy's pitfall of looking for comparisons at the end of a time without having compared things at the start. Leroy and Candy suggest a two-week time period, which shows application of everyday knowledge to the problem.

In this problem there is no control over the growth of nails so it is an information-seeking investigation but one where variables have to be controlled in the way that the measurements or comparisons are made.

How will they use their results to give an answer to the original problem? Candy states carefully that she would need to subtract one set of measurements from the other; Leroy also says how the result would give the answer (though it would only be a valid result if the nails started at the same length). The others say little on this subject; Lisa's suggestion of a block graph is rather as if it were a magic wand.

There are some essential parts of planning that none of these children include—and that are rare in most children's planning. None suggests the equipment they would need to use. Would a ruler be good enough for measuring the small changes in the length of nails? If they had thought about this they might have rejected the whole idea of direct measurement and perhaps cut pieces of paper to fit the nails and compared these with each other instead. None of the plans suggests measuring different toes and fingers to replicate the results, yet the students seem prepared to draw conclusions about toenails and fingernails in general from an implied single set of measurements.

Perhaps this is enough about nails at this point, and enough to show that there is a great deal of thinking—and fun—in working out how to tackle quite a simple problem. Surely one of the important aims of science education is to help children approach problems with this scientific thinking. Planning and carrying out investigations should be closely coordinated, and in practice the planning often takes place, or at least continues, after an investigation has begun. In considering planning separately we do not suggest that it is a separate activity. Rather, it is a neglected one and deserves some consideration in its own right.

The Skills Involved in Planning

Planning concerns the various steps in between raising a question or identifying a problem and supplying an answer. In planning, these steps are thought about and decided rather than carried out in practice. However, the fact that they are to be carried out in practice is important to the process, for planning has to be purposeful.

So we start with a question, which may or may not be expressed as something that can be investigated. If it is not in such a form, the first step is to express it so that it is an investigable question—one that indicates what is to be compared or changed and what to look for as a result. Several investigable questions might come from one initial general one. For example, when some children were going to do some tie-dyeing the question arose: "How do we get the best results when we dye our material?" This is not in an investigable form. As they moved from art to science they had to think what this might mean in terms of evidence to collect. Some of the investigable questions that could be identified from it are

Does the strength of dye make any difference to the color?

Does the time the material is left in the dye make any difference to the color?

Does the type of material make any difference to the color?

Maybe it is only relevant to investigate one of these; in any case, they should be considered one at a time. Having selected one, the next stages concern the identification of the thing or condition to be changed (the independent variable), the things or conditions to keep the same (the variables to be controlled), and the outcome or effect to be looked for (the dependent variable) that gives the results. Then students have to think about how to use the results to answer the original question.

This process may sound rather theoretical, but the following examples should help to show that it is a familiar planning process used when we want to make a "fair test" of something. The steps in the process are not necessarily carried out in a set order. The order varies according to the type of problem. The problem about the dye led to "I wonder what happens if" questions. For one such question, about whether the strength affects the color that is produced, the planning steps are shown below.

General question	How do we get the best results when dyeing?
Investigable question	What happens to the color if we change the strength of the dye?
What should be changed in the investigation? (the independent variable)	The amount of dye dissolved
What should be kept the same? (the controlled variables)	The amount of water, the temperature, the type of material, the time of soaking, and any others that might be thought likely to make a difference
What kind of effect should be observed? (the dependent variable)	The color
How will the result be used to answer the question?	If there is a difference, it will be possible to say what change resulted in a deeper or paler color. If not, the answer will be that changing the strength made no difference in this investigation

So far the planning has been carried out at the level of principle or general strategy. There has been no decision as to how many different strengths of dye will be used, how the other variables will be controlled, and how the depth of color (the dependent variable) will be detected. The plan does not yet show what is to be done, that is, it is not yet operationalized.

The practical limitations on what can be done have to be taken into account, since it is no use preparing a plan that ignores the fact that, say, spectrometers or high-speed cameras are not available in primary/elementary and middle schools. So each step has to be translated into a practical action, as follows:

Planning step	General plan (not operationalized)	Specific plan (operationalized)
What should be changed?	The amount of dye dissolved	At least three different amounts; try four (have we enough dye?)
What should be kept the same?	The amount of water	Measure the amounts or make the same in some other way
	The temperature	Use a thermometer or judge by hand
	The type of material	Make sure pieces are cut from same material
	The time of soaking	Use a clock or dye pieces simultaneously
How will a difference in color be observed?	Compare different pieces of material	If differences are small, get several people to judge and perhaps put them in order of palest to deepest

There are usually several ways of putting a general plan into operation, and part of the skill of planning is to improvise and to overcome practical obstacles. In the dyeing example the lack of, say, a thermometer might pose a problem. This could be overcome by mixing all the dyes at the same time using water from the same source and dyeing all the pieces of fabric simultaneously. This obviously has disadvantages in terms of utensils and organization, but the pros and cons will vary from one classroom to another.

Practical details can often assume such a proportion as to confuse the issue. An important role for the teacher is to make sure this does not happen. It helps in doing this to realize that the various steps in planning are the same from one problem to another. The children will not necessarily realize this, but it is important for the teacher to do so. The general plan is a useful first stage in planning; the second stage is to translate the general plan into a set of actions to be taken.

Suppose the question had been about the rate of bobbing up and down of a toy duck suspended from a spring. The general planning is not too difficult. There are several investigable questions associated with this question and again we take only one (Figure 6–1).

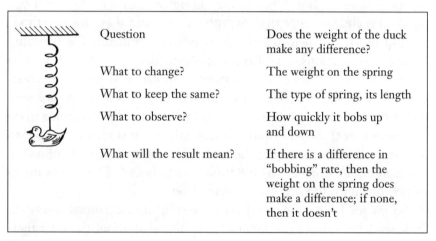

	Question	Does the weight of the duck make any difference?
	What to change?	The weight on the spring
	What to keep the same?	The type of spring, its length
	What to observe?	How quickly it bobs up and down
	What will the result mean?	If there is a difference in "bobbing" rate, then the weight on the spring does make a difference; if none, then it doesn't

Figure 6–1.

The second stage of planning will have to take into account what is possible. How many different weights should be tried? Do they have to be toys? As with the dyes, there should be at least three and ideally four or five different values to the independent variable (the weight on the spring) if a pattern or relationship is being sought. If the length and type of spring needs to be kept the same, how many identical springs are available? If there are no two springs the same, then the various trials will have to be carried out using the same spring, one after another. This has implications for answering the question "How should we measure or compare how quickly the weight bobs up and down?". If there is only one spring, direct comparison is impossible and some timing device is needed. If there is no timer in working order, the problem calls for ingenuity, such as using someone's pulse or watch. There is still the question of what to time. Children's suggestions for this have included:

"the time for twenty bobs"

"one minute and count how many bobs it makes"

"time how long it takes to stop bobbing"

"time how long one bob takes"

These are all worth discussion, which may lead to one or more being eliminated. But if there is not enough evidence to show that one method is clearly better than the others, then the alternative methods should be tried. Such experience is not only valuable for planning future investigations, but also for applying concepts. The child who would measure the rate of movement in terms of its duration probably has not sorted out these two different concepts in his or her own mind and the practical experience may give him or her a chance to do so. Note that this opportunity comes only when students are able to be involved in the planning themselves, not when they are following someone else's instructions to "time twenty bobs." This is a point to which further reference will be made later.

So far we have considered action-testing investigations where an independent variable can be changed. But what about the investigations of questions such as: "Does the moon's phase affect our weather?" "If the daffodils flower early, do all the spring flowers appear earlier too?" "Is the wood at the top of a tree the same as the wood at the bottom?" In these cases there can be no manipulation of the moon or the daffodils or the wood, in contrast to the way in which the strength of the dye could be changed. Nonetheless the problems can lead to investigable questions—and these can be subject to fair testing. Because of the nature of the problem, the planning steps are slightly different from before.

Let's look at the problem of the wood in a tree. This was actually investigated by some children in a school when a tree was felled in the school grounds. The children obviously showed interest in the felling and began to discuss what uses the wood might have. Some said that it would depend which part of the trunk was used because "the wood at the bottom is harder than the wood at the top." They thought this should be so because "the wood at the bottom has to stand all that weight; besides the top wood isn't so old." Not everyone was satisfied by this argument that there must be a difference, so they wanted to find out. The investigation had to be carefully planned because they had to have wood samples sawn off and they had to decide what they wanted. The steps in planning are shown below.

General question	Is the wood the same at different points up the trunk?
Investigable question	Is the wood at the bottom harder than the wood at the top?
What to look at? (dependent variable)	The hardness of the wood
What must be different between the things looked at? (the independent variable)	The part of the trunk from which blocks of wood are taken
What must be the same? (the variables to be controlled)	The direction of grain in the blocks, the position of the block in relation to the bark and the heartwood, etc.
How will the result be used to answer the question?	The results of the same tests on both blocks must be compared to see if the block from the bottom is harder than the block from the top

In an investigation of this kind the greatest difficulty is in making the observations or comparisons. There are no difficult decisions about the independent variable, since there are really no other possibilities. The variables to be controlled might well be controversial because children may not know whether or not certain features affect the hardness. This did happen, for some children mentioned that the blocks should be the same thickness for the test to be fair. To the teacher this seemed to be a misconception of what was meant by "hardness" (mistaking it for "strength") but it was left as a suggested control until they had discussed how the hardness was to be compared.

It was not difficult to find ideas for comparing hardness (in the teacher's and children's books in the classroom); the problem lay in choosing the best tests for the purpose. The teacher suggested that the children should try out some ideas on some other pieces of wood while they were waiting for the workmen to have time to saw off their samples. They tried a hammer-and-nail test, but found that the result depended on who was wielding the hammer, so this wasn't good enough. They finally ended up with a contraption to release a sharpened dart from somewhere near the ceiling to fall on to the block on the floor. Correctly positioning the block presented a challenge, solved eventually by a plumb line (and leading to a considerable interest in how vertical some supposedly vertical surfaces in the room were). The class took care of the safety factor by erecting a corrugated cardboard screen around the block. It was agreed that the depth of penetration of the dart point would be a measure of the hardness of the wood. During this trial of the measuring procedure, the children who said that the thickness of the blocks should be the same realized that this would not matter, but added, "It will if it makes one higher than the other because the dart won't fall so far."

So by far the greatest time in the planning (and performance) of this investigation was spent on defining what to compare or measure and how to carry it out in practice. This planning itself involved practical investigation, as we have seen, but it resulted in a very satisfying test of the original question. Without the careful planning it is quite likely that the blocks from the tree would have been subjected to many inconclusive tests and that motivation would have diminished so that little was learned either from the failures or the successes.

Certainly in this case careful planning paid off. But not without some "trying out." In this case the general plan was straightforward while the specific plan needed more working out both in thought and action. This is not so in all problems and it is often necessary to make a start with an initial plan and modify it along the way. What determines the feasibility of planning beforehand seems to be the complexity of the necessary procedures in relation to the children's ability to "think them through." Very young children are not able to think through an action, unless it is one they are familiar with; they have to do it, and their action and thought go along together. Older children have a greater capacity for thinking through simple actions but still have to "try and see" when faced with unfamiliar or complex sets of actions.

Children's limited experience means that there must be an interweaving of planning and doing. Nothing said here should be taken as a suggestion that children should be kept from starting an investigation until they have produced a plan acceptable to the teacher. But they will learn a great deal about planning by trying to plan and finding out the limitations of their first attempts by putting them into

practice. Gradually they will be able to do more preparation by thinking about the consequences of actions so that not all learning is
through making mistakes.

Interpreting Findings

The value of investigations for helping children's understanding may
be lost if they stop at the point of arriving at results. It all too frequently happens that the physical processes of recording and perhaps
producing a nice-looking table of results is effectively the end of the
activity. But it is very important to reserve time for discussion of the
meaning of the results. For all kinds of investigations, this discussion
should involve returning to the initial question or the original purpose
of the investigation and considering the results in relation to it, as well
as reviewing the way the investigation was carried out. Has the question been answered or the problem solved? What has been learned
that helps develop an understanding of the subject of the investigation? For example, it isn't enough to find that the higher the slope on
which the truck starts, the further it travels; one must also ask why this
might be—what does raising the slope do that makes the truck go further? And finding whether your fingernails grow more quickly than
your toenails is trivial unless it feeds into a developing understanding
of the growth and replacement of cells in living things.

In the case of pattern-finding investigations, there is particular
value in discussing results in order to bring together observations that
might otherwise remain as disconnected findings. The question
"What do you notice about how far the truck rolls and the height of
the end of the ramp?" is likely to produce different kinds of answers,
such as:

1. The higher the ramp, the further it goes.
2. It went the furthest when the ramp was highest.
3. Changing the height changed the distance it rolled.
4. It goes the longest way from the highest and the shortest from the
   lowest.

Each of these is correct, but they don't all encompass the full
sequence of results. In discussion the teacher can find out if those

whose answer was 2 or 4 only took notice of the extreme results or whether they realized that there was a correspondence between all the heights and distances. They might be able to rephrase their answer so that it includes all the results, as in Answer 1. Answer 3 is also incomplete in that it does not say how the two variables are related. Spending some time on such discussion will help children to a greater appreciation of what a pattern means. At all times it is important to check the pattern statements against the evidence. However, it is not helpful to insist upon a certain form of words for expressing a pattern unless children realize the difference between answers of type 1 and other answers.

Exact patterns, where all the evidence obtained fits the pattern, can be used to make predictions, such as predicting how far the truck will roll for a height of the ramp that has not been tried. It is fun to test the prediction in practice, and it will help children to realize the value of finding and expressing patterns as overall statements. Of course, not all patterns are exact, and as children become able to identify patterns they will be able to handle situations where there is an overall relationship but some exceptions to it. For instance, there is a general tendency for taller people to have longer feet, but there will be people with longer feet than someone who is taller than they are. In these cases predictions based on the patterns have to be made cautiously.

For all patterns, too, it is important to avoid the assumption of a cause-effect relationship between the variables that are found to change with one another. As noted on page 67, there is rarely a direct cause and effect. The pattern does not tell us anything about *why* one thing varies with another, and most often there is at least one other factor that is linked to the ones observed. So this adds value to discussing the possible reasons for what has been found and helping children to begin to distinguish between variables that are associated with each other, but not causally, and cases where variation in one thing is a direct effect of changes in another.

Ways of Helping Children's Planning

From the examples given here it is evident that there are many benefits for children in planning their investigation. The amount and kind of thinking involved in deciding how to carry out an investigation extends understanding of both scientific processes and concepts. However, if these benefits are to be realized then children must do the planning and not just follow someone else's plan. There are three main ways in which teachers can provide children with the experience of planning and help them develop their planning skills:

1. by providing opportunities for groups of children to produce plans
2. by giving children a structure to guide their planning
3. by discussing, after an investigation, not just the results, but also the original plan and how it could be improved

Providing opportunities

Children's diet of science-based activities should be a varied and balanced one. It is not necessary or even desirable for the children to propose and plan every investigation for themselves. We have seen that it is a time-consuming process and there will be times when giving children the opportunity for firsthand experience is best done by providing guidance on what to do. If this is provided by work cards, worksheets, or books, the best ones to use will be those that involve the children in thinking about what they are doing. However, these activities will not be developing planning skills, so it is important that not all investigations are ones that have already been set out. Children should have the opportunity at least five or six times a year to plan and carry through an extended investigation, one that might take several lessons to complete and that is genuinely their own. Only in this way will they experience the satisfaction of finding out about things and testing their ideas through their own actions. In this way they are not only learning to investigate but learning to learn.

When children have little or no experience of planning it is important to start developing this skill by working on some simple investigations. These should be ones where the content and context are familiar to the children so that they can focus on the "how" of the investigation. For this purpose the teacher could introduce investigation of questions such as the following, but preferably they should arise from the children's normal science work. Some ideas for starting points for taking children through the steps of planning are:

- Does hot water freeze more quickly than cold water?
- Do road signs show up better if the letters are white on black or black on white?
- Do insulated cups really keep drinks warm?
- Which kind of surface is best for a kitchen countertop?
- Is a plastic carrier bag stronger than a paper one?
- Does a crushed ice cube melt more quickly or more slowly than a whole one?
- Does a soaked bean seed germinate more quickly than one planted without soaking?

Giving a structure

The understanding of what planning means and the skills that it involves will develop gradually; planning becomes a more elaborate activity as experience increases. But at any point in the course of this development, the teacher and the children should have a clear idea of what they should be thinking about and aiming to produce through their planning. The aim is to enable children to plan through the steps suggested earlier. To help achieve this aim, the teacher can "scaffold" the process, just as the development of concepts can be scaffolded, as suggested in Chapter 5.

The most helpful way of scaffolding is to give a structure to children's planning by asking questions that require them to think about what is involved in a fair test. This can be treated at a range of levels. Children of six and seven are able to discuss the "fairness" of a simple test after they have done it; then they gradually become able to think about fairness before doing a test. "Will it be fair if we do this or that?" Taking the idea of fairness further by discussing variables depends upon repeated experience of investigations and should not be hurried.

Thinking about what might vary can only fruitfully be done after observing what can vary in a variety of situations. After all, if you have no idea of what might be important variables, you are unlikely to be able to say what should be controlled—or you might, as many children do, try to control everything in sight. The content of what is being investigated clearly makes a difference. If it is simple and familiar (as in "Which ball bounces highest?") children are more likely to be able to devise a fair test than if the situation is complex or unfamiliar ("Which of these solutions has the highest osmotic pressure?"). So it is important to help children develop planning skills in relation to questions or problems that are meaningful to them. The structure for thinking about variables can be given in several ways. Here is a very useful suggestion that was first proposed in the Science 5–13 unit *Working with Wood* (1972):

> After discussion they might write, on separate cards, each of the things they decide could vary in their investigation. From their collection of cards they could then select the variable they are investigating . . . and line up beside it all the other cards that represent variables that they must try to keep constant. . . .

The further extension proposed is making an experiment planning board as shown in Figure 6–2.

Discussing possible improvements

Children often indicate dissatisfaction with their investigations in terms of the results. When results are inconclusive, or not what they expected, they describe their experiment as "no good." Repeated experience of disappointing activities can reduce motivation, but discussing them can have the double benefit of sharpening self-criticism and reducing the likelihood of the same unfruitful approach being used again. The value of discussion cannot be overemphasized, for planning on its own may otherwise be no more than writing a work card and then following it.

The principal aim of discussing investigations after they have been done is to develop the habit of self-criticism and reflection on the procedures used. Children require help with this and the teacher should vary the degree of support as the children gradually become able to take over the process themselves. As a start, it may be best to talk with children in groups when their investigation has been finished but before the equipment has been put away. The teacher's questions should be open ones, with no critical implication. "How did you decide which masses to add to the truck?" "What results did you get with each one?" "How did you use the results to decide whether the

Support   *Permanent labels made by the children*

Pin board   *Temporary labels pinned on by the children for a particular experiment*

The planning board can be used for any "fair test" type of investigation. It is divided into four parts.

1. Under a permanent label such as "This is our experiment," the children pin up a statement of the question they are investigating (for example, "Which kind of sugar dissolves most quickly?")

2. Under the permanent label "These things might vary," they pin labels on identifying all the things that can vary, both independent variables and variables that should be controlled (for example, the amount of water, the temperature of the water, the kind of sugar, the amount of stirring). Often this list of variables is the result of a group brainstorming.

3. Under the permanent label "We are investigating," they select, as a result of discussion, the one variable that will change in the investigation (in this case, the kind of sugar).

4. Under the permanent label "These things must not vary," they put the other variables, which must not change if the investigation is to be fair (the amount of water, the temperature, the amount of stirring, and any other variable they have identified other than the kind of sugar).

The board then serves as a reminder of their planning while they are conducting the investigation.

Figure 6–2. *Planning board (Science 5–13 1972)*

mass added to the truck made any difference?" Often these kinds of questions are enough to help the children to realize the alternatives that were open to them and the improvements they could have made. If not, then scaffolding questions help to focus on alternative courses of action. "Do you think that you'd find the same results if you added a really big mass to the truck?" The discussion should lead the children to identify the weaknesses in what they did. The teacher's opinion, if offered, should be part of the general pooling of ideas, not a judgment on the success of the work.

When the children become used to reviewing their work, they will not require someone else to help them reflect on what they did, but will do so spontaneously. Then they can respond to questions such as, "How would you change the investigation to improve it if you were starting again?" The implication that it can be improved will not be discouraging when children have reached the point of being self-critical and accepting that there are always different ways of tackling problems and the best way cannot always be foreseen. At this point, too, it is helpful to others to have occasional reporting sessions to the class, where critical comments are invited as each group describes what they have done and found. It is important to see this process as a development and to provide appropriate help for children at different points of it.

Summary of Main Points

This chapter has been concerned with the teacher's role in helping children to plan investigations. Planning skills are important so that children can extend their encounters with the things around them to gather information and ideas in a systematic and satisfying way. Problem-solving ability will improve, too, when children are encouraged to think things out and anticipate useful approaches. Most of all, however, planning skills give children the power to put their own and others' ideas to the test in a scientific way; so they play a central role in developing concepts.

The following different kinds of investigations have been identified, relating to the different kinds of questions that are raised in primary science: information-seeking, action-testing, pattern-finding, and problem-solving.

The nature of planning skills has been described and illustrated by examples. Two levels in planning should be distinguished: the general and the specific. At the general level, the variables have to be identified as those that are to be changed or manipulated (the independent variable), those to be observed or measured (the dependent variable), and those to be kept the same for a fair test (the variables to be controlled). At the specific level, the planning concerns the range over which the independent variable is to be changed, how the measurements or observations are to be made, and the practical steps to be taken to ensure that other variables are controlled.

The interpretation of findings has also been considered since this is central if investigations are to lead to development of conceptual understanding as well as the development of skills.

The development of children's ability to do these things depends on teachers' creating appropriate opportunities and taking action, as summarized in the following suggestions:

1. Keep in mind that children don't learn to plan by being told about planning or following plans devised by others; they must plan for themselves and have opportunities for doing this at least five or six times a year.
2. Look carefully and critically at any worksheets or cards that children use. If these do all the planning for the children, don't use them too often; they prevent children from developing planning skills.
3. Start encouraging children to plan with a fairly simple problem chosen so that you know that they will be able to use their experience to think through what might be done.
4. Provide a structure to scaffold their thinking about the variables to be kept the same, or to be changed, and those to be observed or measured.
5. Organize children to prepare plans in groups so that they combine their thinking.
6. Sometimes discuss plans before the children try them in practice; pool ideas for improving the plans.
7. Always review what was planned after the activity so that experience can be used to improve subsequent planning.
8. Make sure that findings are discussed in terms of the original question or problem and that they think about the meaning of what they found in terms of developing ideas about the subject of the investigation.

Chapter 7

Helping Children to Observe

Observation is a skill of central importance in primary science education, ranking high in the aims and objectives of all primary science programs, in teachers' goals and in what they emphasize in activities. It is used at all stages of inquiry: as a stimulus for raising questions, in linking earlier experience to new encounters, in gathering information (including measurements), in finding patterns and relationships between events and objects. So we shall not spend time making the case for the importance of observation. What we are more concerned about in this chapter is to show that there is a case for helping children to observe more effectively and to focus on the teacher's role in improving children's observation skills.

In this chapter we take a broad view of the meaning of observation and include in it the interpretation or the meaning given to what is observed. The reason for this, as discussed in the first part of the chapter, is that it is not possible to draw a line between observing and interpreting; there is some interpretation from the start. In the second section we look at aspects of the process skill of observing that give it a central role in children's learning in science. The third section brings together some suggestions for actions that teachers can take to help children observe.

About Observation

Observation is the process through which we come to take notice of, become conscious of, things and happenings. It can involve the use of any of the senses—seeing, hearing, feeling, tasting, smelling—alone or in combination. But taking in information by observation is not like soaking up water into a sponge. The senses do not absorb every-thing that is there; they function selectively and the selection is influenced by existing ideas and expectations—even when we taste and smell. For example, wine experts can detect subtleties in these sensations that are lost on those with an uneducated nose and palate. Our existing concepts and knowledge affect what we see or hear or feel. For instance, two people looking at the same formation of clouds in the sky may observe quite different things about them. One, who knows little about clouds except that they block out the sun and bring rain, may see only their extent across the sky and their darkness. Another, who knows the significance of different features of clouds, may be able to report on their probable height, depth, direction of movement, and changing formation, and may be able to predict further changes from these observations.

The story of the vicar and the entomologist walking in the church-yard is another example of how sensing and interpreting coincide. The sound of the choir singing in the church mingled with the whistling of the crickets and other early evening noises of the coun-tryside. The vicar expressed his appreciation of the lovely sound they were hearing. The entomologist agreed: ". . . and it's wonderful to think that it comes from their back legs." Though the physical sounds were available to both, what each heard was different.

In the classroom this means that not everyone observes the same things, even though these things may be there for all to notice. Take the example of the teacher who was hoping to show a group of chil-dren that a candle under a jar would burn for longer the larger the jar. He had three jars of different size and explained to the boys how to put them over three burning candles all at the same time. It worked well. So when the teacher asked them what differences they saw between the jars he was disappointed in their reply: "Nothing. It was same for all of them. All the candles went out." None of the boys had observed what the teacher hoped they would notice—the difference in time of burning in each jar, a difference quite large enough to be noticed by someone looking for it. The teacher might easily have assumed that because the difference was observable it therefore had been observed. We shall discuss later how a teacher might deal with situations of this kind.

What this means is not that we are totally blinkered by what we already know and that we never see beyond it, but it does suggest that developing the ability to observe goes hand in hand with the building of ideas (see also Chapter 1). Developing the process skill of observing enables children to seek consciously for information that will extend their ideas. The teacher's role in this development is to provide opportunities for using the different aspects of observation, often through discussion or through providing problems whose solutions require a wide range of observations to be made and brought together. While this is happening, not only will the children be extending their ideas and understanding of the particular things they observe, but they will also be developing skills that can be applied to other problems and situations. The extension of ideas and understanding is accompanied by a development of the skill of observation and depends to some extent upon it. So there is more to observation than it may seem at first, and if we are to help children to use observation in their science activities it is useful to consider first some aspects that are particularly relevant.

Aspects of Observation

Observing details

A favorite activity of one teacher was to give each child in her class of ten- and eleven-year-olds a lighted candle, firmly secured in a small sand tray, and a blank sheet of paper. The children were asked to write down their observations of the candle flame. Their descriptions varied enormously in detail. Many children were like the one who stopped after writing: "It is yellow and pointed at the top. It flickers." By contrast take the account of another: "The flame is blue at the bottom, turns yellow higher up and tapers to a darker, feathery tip. Inside the whole there is a smaller, darker flame of the same shape. The shape is always changing as the flame flickers." The teacher found that discussing these descriptions led the children back to make more observations, which sometimes settled disputed points but sometimes led to everyone revising and refining their account. She was not so much (in fact, hardly at all) interested in what they learned about the flame, but in what they learned about how much they can find out by looking. Then, when they were looking at other things, which were ones they did want to find out about, she asked them the same kinds of questions as had helped them refine their observations of the candle—about the shape, size, color of each feature; whether it changed or was the same all the time and, if it changed, in what ways and what else changed at the same time; and so on. So, whether it was a caterpillar or a crystal growing in a solution, the children learned to get information from the object by consciously looking in detail at its features.

The value of observing details as opposed to only more global features is that this often helps in making sense of other observations. One child may look at a caterpillar and see that it has seven pairs of legs spread out along its body. Another child may notice the differences between the shape and movement of the three pairs of walking legs and the four pairs of cushion feet. The second child is obviously in a better position to relate the caterpillar's legs to those of the butterfly after metamorphosis and to the generalization that insects have three pairs of legs.

Observing similarities and differences

Children's senses are acute and they are well able to detect small points of difference between two fairly similar objects. They enjoy the quiz book game of "spotting the mistakes" in two pictures that look similar but aren't. But what makes this difficult in a quiz context is not the sensitivity of vision required, it is that the mistakes are totally random. There is no pattern in what one is looking for, and one observation does not give a clue to another. Observation in the context of science activities is not like this. Here there is a purpose to the observation of differences, which is often to detect a set of conditions or properties that helps to explain something or solve a problem. Listing all possible differences confuses the issue and may make a useful pattern more difficult to pick out. For instance, when some children were finding out how to distinguish between eggs that were solid inside and those that were still liquid inside, they first made various observations of differences between eggs known to be cooked and others that were not cooked. They listed differences in movement of the eggs (rolling and spinning), in the sounds they made when tapped, in what happened when the eggs were put in tap water and in salty water, and so on. It would not have helped them for this investigation to have added that the shells were slightly different textures and that one had a blue label and one a red one. Thus children have to learn to distinguish relevant from nonrelevant differences in terms of the problem in hand or the reasons for their observation.

The observation of similarities is really more important than that of differences, yet is not so often given attention. To see that, despite their many differences, the two objects in Figure 7–1 have something in common is to recognize the characteristics that they share that give them a similar function or meaning. If we were unable to do this we would be at a loss to cope with the variety of objects and events that surround us, since we would have to learn about each individually. Picking out the significant features that things have in common from the many ways in which they differ is central to concept formation. Thus the recognition of similarities of certain kinds between things is a skill needed in situations where everything seems to be different. Furthermore, it is important to be able to see that different groupings can be produced by giving attention to different features. So, for example, the cat, dog, and canary fall in the same group if we focus on the observation that these are often found in people's homes, or on the possession of a tail, but fall in different groups if we consider other features of their anatomy or their food.

Figure 7–1. *Despite the differences, these have enough in common for us to identify them both as objects for sitting on*

89

Observing sequence in events

Often it is the relationship between one observation and another, rather than any individual observation, that helps in the understanding of events. For example, a child might observe that there is moisture on a cold can of juice taken out of the fridge. The understanding of why this is so will be helped by making observations in a sequence. Was there moisture on the can when it was in the fridge? When does it appear? What happens if the can is left out of the fridge for a long time? Does it appear if an empty can is used? Similarly, careful observation of the process of colored ink being soaked up by blotting paper helps a child to grasp how the different constituent colors can be separated, so chromatography can become a phenomenon within his or her understanding, rather than something that happens as if by magic.

Detecting patterns in observations

The association of one observation with another has already been mentioned in relation to similarities and differences and sequences. Detecting patterns in observations takes this a step further. Patterns are not found by first making all possible observations and then seeing what relation is to be found; it often requires looking to and fro between the observations and ideas about possible patterns. So we notice what looks like a pattern and then return to make more observations to see if they fit. This is why we often see or hear something more clearly the second time, not because we take in more information, but because we focus on selected parts and cut out the "noise." For example, in the "Newton's cradle" toy (Figure 7–2), if one ball is

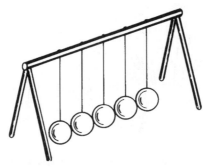

Figure 7–2. *Newton's cradle*

drawn aside and let go, another ball swings away at the opposite end. If two balls are taken together, two swing away. This suggests a pattern, but to verify it, other observations would have to be made. Here the hypothesized pattern is focusing further observation. Similarly, patterns can be established in observations of weather conditions at the simplest level of associating clouds with rain to the more complex patterns used in weather forecasting. The use of patterns in observations for making predictions and for suggesting explanations shows very clearly how this process skill helps in the development of ideas and generalizations that represent our understanding of phenomena in the world around us. (See also Chapter 6.)

Some benefits of observation

Discussion of these aspects of observation shows that using this skill helps children's learning in science in a number of ways, for example:

- Stimulating scientific investigation—noticing similarities and differences can be the stimulus to inquiry. For example, when some children studying bones from various animals noticed that some were different colors, the question "Do different-colored bones come from different animals?" was the start of an investigation.
- Extending knowledge of the world—children have much to learn from close observation about what is in the world around them and how it behaves. Just noticing that a pencil placed in water appears to be thickened under the surface extends knowledge of the properties of water. If, in observing a burning candle, children notice the pool of liquid wax around the wick, they are gathering information relevant to understanding why a candle needs a wick and how it works. And detailed observation of the natural world cannot fail to bring awareness of the rich diversity of plants and animals. When some children were given small patches of a field to examine, the teacher found the same reaction from all the groups: they were amazed at the number of different plants in such a small area.
- Drawing conclusions from investigations—observation has a particularly important part to play here, since the quality of observations made is a significant factor determining whether meaningful conclusions can be drawn. Children observing that a spiral of thin

cardboard rotates when suspended over a candle flame often have to be helped to recognize that noticing the way the spiral turns is crucial to the conclusion that can be drawn about what happens to air when it is heated. Does the movement of the spiral mean that the air is moving upwards? Why not downwards? To answer this means looking again not just at whether the spiral turns, but in which direction, and finding out if this is consistent with air moving upwards through it. The attempt to use evidence in this way sends children back to make more observations and so refines this skill while making use of it.

- Conceptual development—picking out what is similar when many things are different—assists in developing and broadening concepts. To do this means that observations have to be brought together and connected with each other, not left as isolated observations. This has to happen not just in observing things that are together, such as the objects in Figure 7–1, but also across time and in different places. For example, a teacher demonstrated the condensation of water vapor from a boiling kettle onto a cold plate. In discussion the children were able to relate this observation to the fogging of the windows in the kitchen when vegetables are being boiled and to the misting of the mirror in the bathroom when a bath is being run. From these observations they could pick out what was similar about the conditions in which water vapor was condensed and this helped them understand the process of condensation.

The Teacher's Role

Activities designed specifically to give children practice in observing, such as the observation of a candle flame (page 87), should be rare events. If used too frequently they defeat their own end, since they quickly become boring and provoke an unthinking routine reaction. For the most part, observation is best developed in the activities in which it is used. As we have seen, it serves various purposes in inquiry, and the value of the inquiry for learning depends partly on the quality of observation. So how can teachers encourage effective observation?

1. By providing opportunity and invitations to observe
2. Allowing time for careful and detailed observation
3. Asking appropriate questions to focus observation
4. Enabling students to extend their range of observations
5. Discussing what is observed

Opportunity for observation

Opportunity means that there is access to appropriate materials and events with the time to make observations in detail and in depth and, if necessary, to repeat and refine them. The materials for observation should be selected so that observations can be made that are relevant to the concepts or generalizations the teacher has in mind. This does not mean highly structured "set pieces," but that some thought is given to the materials. For example, children may understand a great deal more about the development of fruits and seeds if they are able to observe fruits at different stages of maturity than if they are given only one fruit to examine. They might be asked to try to put the fruits in a sequence of maturity and to say what features led them to choose that sequence. Through this they can find out firsthand about the changes that accompany the development of seeds.

Materials relevant to a topic (such as the fruits just mentioned) can be displayed on a side table for a few days before the topic is a subject for activities in science lessons. It may help to include with these materials some "invitations to observe"—cards that ask, "What do you notice about _____ ?" "How are these _____ different from these _____ ?" "What's the same about these _____ ?" "What happens when you put _____ and _____ together?" and so on. The teacher might also make some time for a whole-class discussion of what has been observed in response to these questions, in this way underlining the value of observing and the importance the teacher attaches to it.

Asking children to draw often encourages them to pay attention to detail if the situation is set up to require them to do this. For example, before some children went out to observe grasshoppers, their teacher asked them to try to draw a grasshopper from memory as well as they could. As soon as they began, they realized what they did not know about grasshoppers and so they eagerly took the opportunity to find out these things from observation.

Time for observation

Time is an important dimension in providing opportunity to observe. A short period of free observation or of free play with the materials is a most effective way of stimulating children to raise questions, to wonder about things. The period allowed should not be too long; about ten minutes is sufficient. Many children seem to observe only superficially and to lose interest within minutes. But these same children often return to the objects after the chance to think and particularly after discussion. For example, the boys who at first saw no difference among the candles under the different-sized jam jars were fascinated by their "discovery" when their teacher asked them to look particularly at whether the candles all went out at the same time when the experiment was repeated. Then they wanted then to do it again and again, and each time they became more sure of what they saw.

Extending the range of observations

Development in observation skill shows in the ability to use equipment to extend the range of our senses. These include simple things such as hand lenses, thermometers, and bifocal microscopes. To this we must add the use of computers and sensory probes. In all these cases the children need to know how to use the equipment correctly and how to interpret what they see. The use of computers with data-logging software and sensing probes has extended the range of senses other than sight and increased the sensitivity of observation. This means that children can observe, for example, small differences in temperature of different parts of their skin, or the change in light intensity as light passes through a colored filter (helping children to realize that something is taken away, not added, when white light turns into colored light). Computer logging also enables data to be collected when children are not present. For example, children studying the change in the length of a day across seasons were able to record the level of light in the classroom over a complete twenty-four hours and compare this in summer and winter. Using the same equipment they were also able to identify the exact times of sunrise and sunset and to see how this varied throughout the year.

It is important, of course, for children to be able to know what the probes are measuring and what the lines or bars on the computer screen mean. It's useful to begin to introduce computer data-logging with a situation where the familiar equipment and the new can be used side by side; for instance, to have a thermometer and a temperature probe in warm water as it cools and to see that the instruments are detecting the same thing. The teacher has an important role throughout in checking on the meaning that the children are giving to what they see on the computer screen.

Teachers' questions

Questions of various kinds, discussed in Chapter 3, are used to get children started into an inquiry. During an activity teachers can use questions phrased specifically to encourage children to use process skills, including observation. Suppose children are investigating "What happens if we make pancakes with self-rising flour instead of plain flour?" Without prompting, it may be that the children will look for differences between the pancakes made with different flours only at the end of the exercise—in the taste, probably. With some careful questions, though, they may be alerted to look for differences in the events, at each stage in the making: What do you notice that is the same in the two mixtures before cooking? What is different? What can you hear? (possibly bubbles rising and popping in one of the mixtures). These questions can be repeated to focus observations during cooking and again after, not just at the end. Then observations are more likely to lead to a realization of the part rising agents play in the cooking process through seeing the bubbles that appear when the mixture made with self-rising flour is heated.

Teachers' questions have another role during the activities. Ideally the teacher should be observing how the children carry out their inquiry, but (s)he cannot be in several places at once. Inevitably when coming to talk with each group about how they are progressing, the teacher will not know whether the students have observed certain details, which may be critical. In such cases the questioning should be aimed at a recapitulation of the evidence gathered. If unexpected results are reported, the teacher should ask for a "replay," whenever this is possible, without suggesting that what the children have said is "wrong." Take the case of the group measuring the relative strength of threads of different kinds. They told the teacher that the thickness of the thread made no difference to the strength. To the question, "Tell me, how did you decided that?" they replied, "Well, when we hung six hundred grams on the thick one, it broke and the same with the thin one." In this case, imperfect experimental technique prevented them from making the observations that the teacher had expected them to make. It often happens that children just do not observe the things we may assume that they have observed. This is because we, as adults, know that the opportunity for the observation is there, but for various reasons what the children have observed may be subtly different. Thus the teacher has a key role in using "focusing" questions (see page 27) to ensure that children take notice of the things that will help their understanding.

Discussion of observations

Discussion is important in all aspects of inquiry, as we discuss in Chapter 8. In relation to observation, discussion can be used to serve the same function in a group as drawing does on an individual basis, that is, it heightens awareness of what information the children can obtain by observation. For example, a class was being taken to visit a church to look in particular at the signs of age and weathering of stone. The teacher prepared them beforehand by asking them where they thought the stone would be most worn, how they would recognize weathering and wearing away, in what ways they thought old stones would differ from newer stones, and so on. During the discussion, children did not necessarily agree on any of these points, which increased the children's interest in going to see for themselves. They made observations which they almost certainly would not have been made without the focusing effect of the discussion.

Discussion of observations requires some organization, however. Good discussions don't just happen; they need planning. Some of the ways in which they can be set up and managed are discussed on page 101. When children are reporting and discussing observations, some structure is needed, for the range of comments on different aspects means that the exchange can easily become disorganized. In a class discussion among six- and seven-year-olds the children were bubbling over to tell what they had seen following a session observing mealworms. The discussion could easily have become disjointed, with comments on various aspects of mealworm structure and behavior following one another in quick succession. Instead, the teacher kept the subject to the observation made by the first child to report. This concerned the number of legs the mealworms had, and other children were invited to add comments about this while new topics were kept at bay. There was a considerable bonus in doing this, since it emerged that some children thought the mealworms had three legs, others that they had six legs, and others claimed to have seen eight legs. So this discussion turned out to be a considerable stimulus to further observation, focused on this particular point, and the later observations made were far more detailed and accurate than on the first occasion.

These approaches to encouraging children to observe clearly overlap and will in any case generally be used in combination. The emphasis on one or another approach will depend on how well-developed are the children's observation skills. We discuss the matter of finding and using information about this development in Chapter 9.

Summary of Main Points

Observation has been discussed as an important means by which we gather information directly from the world around us. We have noted that observation is conceptually driven and that our senses respond selectively, not comprehensively, to signals from our environment. Thus observation is not the same as just looking; children capable of seeing detail and detecting sequences in events often fail to notice these things unless they are pointed out. This adds force to the point that observation is not the same as using the senses; what we take in is influenced by existing ideas, expectations, and how we view a particular task.

Key aspects of observation relevant to developing children's scientific understanding have been considered: noticing details, finding similarities and differences, identifying the sequence in events, and detecting patterns and relationships. Discussion of these has revealed the contribution that observation makes to conceptual development through stimulating inquiry, extending knowledge, and helping children to interpret and draw conclusions from their findings.

Thus observation is a skill that children can and need to develop so that they can more effectively learn directly from the objects and materials around them. In doing so they may become more effective in grasping concepts, proposing investigations, gathering relevant data, and drawing conclusions from their inquiries.

The teacher's role in helping the development of observation skill involves providing opportunity and encouragement to observe, ensuring that there is enough time to go beyond superficial observations, asking questions to focus observations, helping students to extend their range of observations, and discussing what has been or could be observed. Actions teachers can take to ensure that observation skills are developed can be summarized as follows:

1. Give children sufficient time to observe something; when new material is introduced, allow a period of free play before starting to discuss or focus observations.
2. After the initial period of observation, as appropriate, help children to go beyond superficial features and into detail, by asking "focusing" questions or requesting drawings or descriptions of particular features.
3. Provide plenty of material for children to handle and observe at all times, not just in science lessons, and use displays with labels that invite children to observe and explore what is there.
4. Give thought to the selection of materials so that, by observation, children are able to find differences and similarities, sequences in events, and evidence on which to base tentative conclusions.
5. Organize observation activities, so that children can talk in groups about what they find, and whole-class discussions in which groups or individuals tell the rest of the class what they have observed.
6. Sometimes provide a stimulus for observation by discussing events or objects beforehand, so that the children are ready to look out for certain kinds of evidence or information (particularly relevant when observation time is limited, as on a visit).

7. Take care in deciding the kind of question to pose as a stimulus to children's observation; broadly focused questions have the merit of allowing children to decide for themselves what to observe, but narrowly focused ones have their place in cases where there is something special that the children might miss.

Chapter 8

Helping Children to Communicate

If we have to nominate the three most important aspects of a teacher's role in primary science, the most likely candidates would be providing materials for children to observe and investigate (Chapters 6 and 7), asking the right kinds of questions (Chapters 3 and 4), and helping children to discuss or, more widely, to communicate their thinking and developing ideas. Communication is a vital aspect of the progress of science. It can take various shapes, but never the shape of a teacher dictating summaries, nor of a child chanting memorized answers. In this chapter we consider communication of three kinds, which are central to children's learning in science: various types of discussion; using notebooks (journals) or folders; and drawing, painting, and modeling.

Discussion

Whole-class discussion

A class discussion or "class conversation" often takes place after some work has been accomplished and before activities are resumed, or new ones initiated. The beginning of a lesson is often the best time for a whole-class discussion since, once the children are off on to new explorations, it can be difficult to bring them together, or to catch their attention. It's best to try not to interrupt them at awkward moments, just when things are beginning to happen. But occasionally this will be needed, if work threatens to veer off in a wrong direction and the teacher has to interfere. To avoid this it's helpful to plan with the children at the start of a lesson that they will stop working at a certain time in order to compare notes and to report to each other. Then the children will then know what to expect.

A class conversation is a form of communication where ideas are openly shared. Handled well, it kindles new interests, invites the testing of new ideas that the children put forward, challenges others' work, proposes possible answers to remaining problems, or opens up new lanes of discovery and exploration. The teacher's comments and ideas should be offered and accepted in the same way as the children's, that is, because they are useful and convincing because they are based on evidence available to everyone—not because they have more authority. The discussion also gives the teacher a chance to make unobtrusive corrections, to give further encouragement, to point out relationships, to highlight what is relevant, and to obscure what is trivial. The children's own contributions often have great impact on each others' thinking; they challenge each other more effectively than the teacher by insisting on clarity of explanation, or by comparing results of similar, or repeated, experiments. Children correct each other by conviction, not through obedience.

This positive, helping atmosphere (see also Chapter 2) will not be created without some structure. People have to listen in conversations, as well as speak, and it is up to the teacher to manage the exchange so that those taking part have equal say and equal chance both to ask and to answer questions. This role in relation to the structure of the discussion does not mean that the teacher dominates or determines the content of the exchanges. Acting rather like a chairman, the role is to help the discussion keep to one subject until everyone has said what they have to say about it. This will often mean delaying some comments brought up on a different topic and the teacher must remember to return to them at a later point.

It is also worth arranging the class in a way that fosters participation in the discussion. Depending on the number and size of the children and the shape and size of the room, it may be helpful to bring the children to one part of the classroom, perhaps having them sitting on the floor, as they might do when listening to a story. This focuses attention on the shared topic and encourages children to take part and throw some ideas into the exchange. It is difficult for some children to muster the courage to speak if they are physically separated from the teacher by what seems to them an enormous distance.

Small-group discussion with the teacher

Discussion between the teacher and small groups or individuals usually takes place while activities are in progress. On this account the teacher has to judge carefully when and, if so, how to intervene. Children usually delight in showing or describing what they are doing or what they have discovered or accomplished. They chat incessantly among themselves, or to nobody in particular, but they easily make the teacher a partner of the conversation, provided they have something about which to communicate. If they are not ready to communicate, then they are better left alone for a while. It is all too easy to spoil things for children by poor timing. Jos Elstgeest recalled this event that he observed in a classroom:

> Anna was a rather shy little girl. She was not yet very confident in herself. She was working with a ruler. Something was going on. The teacher happened to pass her and, in his eagerness, wanted her to talk about her work.
>
> "What are you doing, Anna?" he asked.
>
> Anna did not reply. She started fiddling with her ruler and stopped whatever she was doing. The interruption was just too much for her at this stage of her work. But this teacher would not give up and insisted: "Are you measuring something?"
>
> "Yes," whispered Anna.
>
> "What are you measuring?"
>
> "...???...[giggle]...???"
>
> "Are you measuring your desk or your book?"
>
> "Yes."

This conversation makes it plain that, if the teacher had asked Anna, "Are you measuring the moon?", she would have promptly whispered "Yes." The odds are that Anna was not measuring anything at all! Why didn't the teacher leave Anna alone? The conversation did not make him any wiser, and it put Anna completely off whatever she was doing. Eventually she would have shown signs of wanting to share her work with somebody, perhaps by showing it to a friend, or, perhaps, by drawing a picture or writing something in her workbook.

Such unhelpful interventions can be avoided by joining the group to listen and get a feel for what is going on before asking questions. For example:

> Deidre and Allyson were investigating the way in which three whole hens' eggs, labeled A, B, and C, behaved in tap water and in salty water. They knew that one was hard-boiled, one soft-boiled, and one raw. They had to find out which was which. The transcript begins with the teacher approaching them after they had been working alone for some time.

DEIDRE: ... hard-boiled.

ALLYSON: I know.

TEACHER: (coming up to them) Can you tell me how you're getting on?

DEIDRE: I think that C is raw.

ALLYSON: We both think that C is raw.

TEACHER: Do you?

DEIDRE: B is ...

TEACHER: (to Allyson) Why do you think that?

ALLYSON: Because when you put eggs in water bad ones rise to the top.

DEIDRE: (at the same time) Because it ... we put them all in. . . .

TEACHER: Bad?

ALLYSON: Yes, I think so—or it is the good ones? . . . well, I don't know.

TEACHER: Yes?

ALLYSON: ... they rose to the top, so . . .

> (Deidre is putting the eggs into the salty water.)

DEIDRE: ... that's the bottom. (Pointing to C.)

ALLYSON: ... if it's raw it should stay at the bottom.

TEACHER: I see.

DEIDRE: So that's what we think, C is raw and B is medium, and A is hard-boiled. (Allyson starts speaking before she finishes.)

ALLYSON: ... and I think that B is hard-boiled and she thinks that B is medium.

TEACHER: Ah, I see. (to Deidre) Can you explain, then, why you think that?

DEIDRE: If we put... er... take C out, (She takes C out, puts it on the table, then lifts A and B out.) and put these in, one after the other. Put A in—no, B first. That's what ... Allyson thinks is hard-boiled, I think it's medium. If you put that in ... (She puts B into the salty water.)

ALLYSON: . . . 'cos it comes up quicker.

DEIDRE: It comes up quick. And if you put that in . . .

(She puts A into the salty water. It goes to the bottom and rises very slowly.)

ALLYSON: And that one comes up slower.

DEIDRE: So, I think that one (pointing to A) is hard-boiled because it's . . . well . . .

ALLYSON: I don't. I think if we work on the principle of that one (pointing to B). Then that one comes up quicker because it's, you know, not really boiled. It's like a bit raw.

TEACHER: A little bit raw.

ALLYSON: So, therefore, it'll come up quicker.

DEIDRE: Yes, but it's not bad.

TEACHER: What'll it be like inside?

ALLYSON: Runny.

TEACHER: It'll be runny still, I see.

(Adapted from Harlen 2000b, 108)

Here the teacher approached the pair with the aim of checking on progress and asking questions that encouraged the girls to think aloud and so respond to each other's ideas. It is in the small-group situations that the teacher can ask questions that require children to use their process skills—the "What do you think will happen if . . . ?", "What will you do to find out if . . . ?", and "How did you decide that . . . ?" questions and others suggested in earlier chapters.

Small-group discussion without the teacher

There is also discussion among members of a working group when the teacher is not present. This is probably the most important kind of discussion of all, for here children are free to exchange, with equals, even the most seemingly farfetched or half-formed ideas. And by listening to others' ideas, they realize that there are different ways of thinking about and explaining things. They will argue and challenge others' views and have to defend their own. Eventually they may as a group come to a position or hold a view different from the starting point of any of them. Their combined thinking has produced something better than any individual's thinking. They will have learned that an idea is no use unless there is evidence for it. The kind of evidence that is needed to stand up to the logical prodding of their peers also becomes apparent to each one.

A great deal has already been said in earlier chapters about the value of discussion in fostering the development of particular skills and ideas. Much of this draws upon or refers to the work of Douglas Barnes (1976), who argued eloquently that children's thinking and talking are intimately connected. By studying what children said to each other when involved in group tasks without a teacher present, Barnes found that they contributed to a collective understanding of an event. One child's idea is taken up and elaborated by another, is perhaps challenged by someone else's idea, and leads them back to check with the evidence or to gather more evidence to test alternative ideas. With several minds at work there is less chance of ideas being tested in a superficial manner than if children work alone with no one to challenge their actions or their reasoning. But the challenge can only be made if the thinking is made public through talking. Consequently, Barnes claimed, the more children can "think aloud" in informal discussions, the more they can take the responsibility for formulating their own ideas. When the teacher is not present they cannot depend upon the "right" answer being supplied (if they will only wait long enough), they have to struggle to find their own solutions.

Many teachers worry that when children are working in groups, they cannot adequately supervise all the groups at once. If they can only be one place at a time, how can the other groups be taught? The answer is that the other groups will be learning in a way that they cannot do if the teacher is with them and that this is a most valuable kind of learning. Indeed it is just as well that the teacher cannot be with every group all the time, otherwise children would not have the opportunity of discussion without the presence of "an authority." Absence of this presence frees them, and obliges them, to think aloud and have their thinking criticized by others.

Children's Notebooks/Journals

This section concerns the use of workbooks, folders, journals, or notebooks for children to keep their own notes and make some record of the work. Some of it will be in the form of drawings and painting, discussed further in the next section. Here we focus on the value of using notebooks and ways of encouraging this, avoiding the tedium of "writing up" that spoils the excitement of science activities for so many children.

Work/notebooks are a very special, essential means of communication, too often neglected or underestimated in value. Notebooks used well give not only stability and permanence to children's work, but also purpose and form. They are a record, an extension of their mental activities, a paper memory, a store of personally valued information. Notebooks can contain such unsayable things as drawings, tables, or graphs and are an essential item in the children's scientific tool bag. They may start to use notebooks at a very early stage in their scientific career, even before they know how to write. Drawings are a means of self-expression but, even before that, the discovery that pencils make lines, that ink makes blots, that crayons leave colored tracks and that paints leave lovely smears, is an early form of recording on paper.

As is the case with all other skills and abilities, children need time and plenty of opportunity to practice in order to develop their skill of self-expression, which will gradually improve so as to become real communication. In the earliest stages, children want a notebook to draw what they see and to write or draw about what they think is going on. It may well be that only they, themselves, understand these scribbles and sketches. The drawings may well diverge from reality and be filled with imaginative additions and embellishments; they will be naturally clumsy and childish in comparison with the artistic illustrations in books, but that is how it should be, for the notebooks are the children's own, while the printed books are not.

Later, notebooks become useful instruments for recording what they do in their investigations and the results they get. The teacher must take care that the children learn to record what they actually see and do, and not what they think the teacher expects them to have seen or done. Sooner or later the children will have to record data so as to be able to compare results of inquires which require intervals of time. The earlier the children start to learn to keep records, the better they will be prepared to make it an integral part of their science activities. The nature of the notes to be taken depends, of course, on the kind of observation, investigation, or experiment being done. Especially at later stages, it will become necessary to note times or distances or data on other measurements, as soon as they are taken or verified, because interpretation of such data requires a running record. Children themselves will soon recognize from experience (of not doing it) the need for such sustained records.

Using a notebook or making some kind of record should become a normal part of science work; but interrupting children in the middle of an activity to insist on their writing something will not achieve this end. It is better to wait till they feel satisfied that they have "done" something, and really have something to write about. It is of the utmost importance for the teacher to realize and to acknowledge that the children's science notebooks are their own workbooks, and not the teacher's trap to test them. Too often the children associate their notebooks with the exercise of "answering the teacher's questions." This does not mean that the teacher may not look at the books in order to detect the children's progress (we deal with this in Chapter 9). Children use their notebooks to express themselves and to communicate; they are like mirrors. They help the teacher to know what the children have thought about, how they have thought about it, what they have observed, what they have or have not understood, and, above all, what they have been, or still are, interested in. These notebooks also help the teacher to recognize which children can work independently and imaginatively and which ones need more encouragement and attention.

Where a sound relationship has been established, and where children are relaxed and confident in their work, they talk freely with and listen to their teacher. Likewise they become aware that they can communicate with their teacher through their notebook as well. Once this relationship has been established, the teacher can add comments to the children's work in the notebooks and the children will accept this as a matter of course. For example, the teacher may suggest a new word to use. When a child writes, "My piece of chalk floats on the water and bubbles come out. Then it goes to the bottom," the teacher may add, "It sinks." Or, coming back from a field trip, a child notes, "I saw an insect and it pushed a ball of cow droppings." Here the comment, "Cow droppings are called 'dung,' and the insect is called a 'dung beetle'" would be in place. These sorts of remarks, instead of leaving a feeling of failure, give encouragement to the children who often want to know the right word, simply because they are keen to express themselves well and clearly.

Another way of helping children is to make suggestions on how to clarify their thoughts, or how to organize their notes. Useful little hints, like drawing dividing lines, preparing a table to collect measurements or observations, numbering recordings of separate experiences, or connecting part of a drawing to its label can be given or inserted in their notebooks whenever it seems desirable. Children's understanding can profit from the teacher's helpful remarks in order to improve their skills of recording. Even suggesting a certain pattern as a model for recording will do no harm, provided there remains flexibility and choice enough to fit any circumstance.

It often happens that children's written records are incomplete, their illustrations less accurate than desirable. How does the teacher correct these shortcomings? In a nutshell, the answer is by not correcting anything. Correction is the children's responsibility and not the teacher's. The latter, however, sees what is needed and helps the children so that they make their own corrections. The approach is illustrated in this example:

> Maria, quietly working with her balance, chose a pile of cotton wool and a small rubber [eraser]. She placed them both on her balance and was surprised that the tiny rubber was heavier than the big fluff of cotton wool. She called her teacher to come and see. He showed interest and talked to her. Maria demonstrated how she came to her unexpected conclusion. "See? The rubber goes down and the cotton goes up." Then the teacher asked her, "Can you find something that is lighter than the cotton wool?" and went his way. Maria tried several objects until she found a peanut which was lighter than the cotton wool. She took her book and wrote, "I put cotton on one side and my rubber on the other. When I put a peanut, the cotton went down." When her teacher saw this cryptogram he gave the following comments. To the first part he added, "What did your balance look like?" and by the second part he asked, "Where did you put the peanut?"

This teacher effectively helped Maria to make her notes better without creating fear or tension. It did not take Maria long to add her drawing of the balance with the cotton up and the side with the rubber down. She also wrote, "The rubber was heavier. Then I put a peanut instead of the rubber, and the peanut was lighter." And this she illustrated with a fresh drawing of the balance in reverse position. And what is more, she thought it was all her own idea!

The tape recorder or "audio notebook"

The use of a tape recorder, acting as an "audio notebook," should be mentioned here. The teacher can introduce it as a way of helping children become aware of the value of making some kind of record of events as they happen. A group might switch on a tape recorder, say for ten minutes, during an activity when they are watching something and talking to each other about what is happening. They can then listen to the recording to refresh their memories of all that happened. For some children who labor over writing, the frequent use of the tape recorder may be appropriate, while for others it should be used more selectively; the children can help decide when it is the best form of recording to use.

Occasional tape recording of group work has an additional benefit for the teacher, who, through listening to a group discussion, can pick up clues to the children's ideas and reasoning expressed in his or her absence. If a recording is replayed with the teacher and group listening together there is the chance of challenging the ideas and of offering alternatives, as suggested in Chapter 5.

Notebooks, visual or aural, have a valuable role in science education for both the children and their teacher. They provide information about the children's ideas and interests and increase the children's interest and ability in recording their work. They should become an integral part of their scientific activities.

Drawing, Painting, and Modeling

It is very common for teachers to involve children in drawing, and sometimes in painting and modeling, as part of science activity. Some drawings will be in children's notebooks but others may be produced as part of a formal record of an activity, perhaps produced by a group in collaboration. Among the various reasons that have been proposed for drawing in science, the most common are that it will help children to observe, remember, and communicate; also, just as with children's notebooks, teachers can use the products to understand the children's thinking better. We consider each of these in turn.

Although there is no indisputable evidence to support the commonly held claim that making some representation of an object will improve observation, it does seem reasonable to suppose that if children are going to record their observations in some way they are likely to observe more closely. Most children in the primary/elementary school do not produce drawings that attempt to represent truly the objects in front of them. Instead their drawings are influenced by prior conceptions about the object. This is illustrated by an investigation of children's drawings of leaves. The children approached the task in the belief that it was important to record accurately the detail of the leaf edge but less important to record the venation accurately. Not surprisingly, their drawings showed more attention to some features than to others. Younger children, when asked to draw several leaves, ceased to observe the actual leaves after awhile and included a stem in their drawings of an elm leaf although no stem was actually visible on the leaf. These children were responding to the leaves in front of them as symbolic leaves. Stems and shapes are particularly prominent in young children's conceptions of leaves and so became the important part of what they "saw." Similar findings were reported from a study of children's drawings of apples by Tunnicliffe (2001), where children were found to add a stalk and leaves that were not present on the apple that they were drawing but are often found on drawings of apples found in books.

Thus if children are left to their own devices they become engrossed in their drawing or painting and stop observing the details of the objects they are representing. Consequently there will be no certain improvement in observation through the activity. The question then arises as to whether the teacher can or should do anything about this, and if so, what?

If the purpose is to record details for use in science inquiries, then it is appropriate to take action to help children shed their preconceptions and really see what is there. The teacher might to do this by drawing attention to particular features of an object that relate to the purpose of the drawing or model. Children watching water birds feeding on a visit to a pond might be asked to look carefully at the birds' beaks and then at the beaks of small birds feeding on the crumbs thrown on the grass around the pond. How would you describe the shape of a duck's bill, when it is open and when it is closed? How is it different from a pigeon's bill? Could a pigeon manage with a duck's bill and vice versa? When the children sit down, there and then on the grass, not later in the classroom, to draw the birds, the beaks might well be drawn more realistically than the rest of the duck.

A great deal of what was said in Chapter 7 is relevant here, for the ways suggested for helping children to observe carefully serve equally to help them represent significant details relating to perception rather than preconception. It is worth reflecting on the word *significant* in this context for a moment, reminding ourselves that it is important for the drawing or painting or modeling to have some purpose. To serve that purpose not all details will be relevant, and therefore a photographic representation or accurate model is not necessarily the most useful. What we mean by "accurate" is that which helps understanding of a particular point. If the ducks' beaks in a child's drawing show that they help in water feeding, then it may not matter that their tails are the wrong shape.

The second reason mentioned earlier for encouraging children to draw, paint, or model was that it will help them remember what they have seen. Certainly research evidence supports the notion that children will remember their own reconstructions of objects and events. However, the value of this will obviously depend upon whether the representations are merely following preconceptions or whether they reflect an attempt to focus upon and understand some part of the object or event.

Similarly the third reason, helping communication, sends us back to the same points about purpose and focus. Figure 8–1 shows the drawings produced by two children when asked, without teacher intervention, to draw a sheep's bone (a vertebra from its spine). The children have made different decisions about what should be communicated. The first child has produced a drawing that accurately reflects the shape of the bone from one perspective. However, the drawing does not show the cavity through which the spinal cord passes. The second child has decided that two drawings are needed, both showing the spinal cord cavity but one from the "front" and one from the "back."

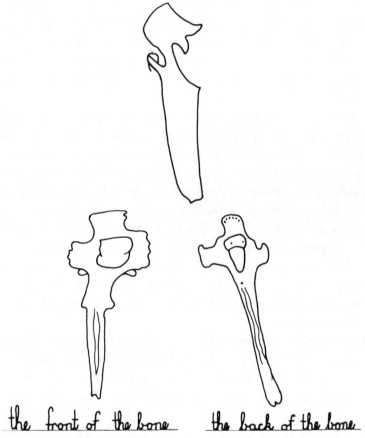

the front of the bone   *the back of the bone*

Figure 8–1. *Children's drawings of bones*

Neither of the children has given a clue as to the relationship between the size of the drawing and the size of the actual bone. This may or may not be important, depending on the purpose of the drawing. If the drawing is to show the general shape of vertebrae in one particular section of the spine of a sheep or to show the way in which the spinal cord is protected, there is no need to mention the actual size of the bone. However, in other circumstances, the size of the bone could be significant.

There are many ideas and skills intervening between seeing something and producing some graphic or plastic representation of it. There is the perception, the taking in of the general scene, the recall of and reaction to previous ideas, the focusing, the questioning, the search for clues to help understanding of what is there, the selection of the medium to use for recording, the struggle to make the marks that fit the intention, the passing to and fro between the ideas, the object, and the image. The teacher can help with all of these through discussion that links the purpose with the observation and with the medium through which it can be communicated. The latter, the medium, brings us to an area of overlap between science education and art education.

Children are not in the same position as an artist; they cannot know what a brush, chalk, pencil, charcoal, or waxed scraper board can do until they have experimented with it. Just as the teacher intervenes to stretch the vocabulary of children, so intervention is appropriate to extend the range of materials and instruments the children can use to develop their graphic skills. A pencil alone can produce a range of different marks. A teacher giving children small pieces of paper to cover in pencil marks of as many different kinds as they can is opening children to new ways of expressing their observations. This serves both to develop graphic skills and observational skills.

So, in summary, before embarking on a drawing or model, discussion between teacher and children should help the children decide about:

1. the purpose, perhaps to excite, to inform, to show something that is beautiful or an interesting pattern
2. the general form or details to focus upon
3. the choice of materials suited to the amount of detail and the general impression to be conveyed
4. how their existing ideas may influence what they produce

Bringing these out into the open may clear the way for seeing things that were there but not previously noticed (such as the pattern of veins and the texture of the surfaces of leaves as well as their size and shape).

Using children's representations as clues to their thinking

Researchers and teachers alike have recently exploited more and more the products of children's drawing, painting, and modeling as a diagnostic tool, since they expose children's thinking. In Chapter 5, drawings were used to give evidence of children's ideas. Figure 8–2 is a further illustration. After demonstrating how water vapor coming from a bottle condenses on a cold plate, this child's teacher went on to explain the water cycle using the demonstration as an analogy. After the class discussion the children were asked to draw the water cycle. As can be seen from the presence of the kettle in the picture drawn by this child, she has not been able to disentangle the analogy used and the water cycle in nature.

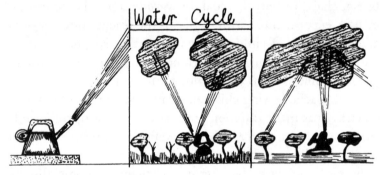

Figure 8–2. *A child's drawing of the water cycle*

Drawings, with annotations written by the child or by the teacher during discussion by the child, enable children to convey how they see things more easily than they can using only words. It is interesting to ask children to draw pictures to show how, for example, they think the dew forms on the grass overnight, what they think happens to food and drink that we swallow, what happens when you turn a water tap on, what keeps a floating boat up and a sunken wreck down in the water. Two points deserve emphasis in the context of children's drawings in science. First, it should be clear that the interest is in what the children think, not just in what is there to be drawn. So, rather than asking children to draw the eggs in Figure 5–2 (page 51), the teacher asked them to draw "what you think is inside the eggs." The second point is the importance of discussing the drawings so that the teacher does not misunderstand what the child is trying to represent.

The question underlying the teacher's role is whether children should be left to discover on their own the various connections between real objects and representations of them. Children's graphic skills develop through well-defined stages, and, as with the stages of cognitive development, there is a limit to how much the development can be accelerated, but there is nonetheless a strong case for teacher intervention. The teacher's role is to help children extend and elaborate these skills, taking account of the stage they have reached, and so use them effectively in exploring and building their understanding of the world around them.

Summary of Main Points

In this chapter we have considered the teacher's role in developing children's ability to communicate as an integral part of their learning in science. The three forms of communication considered here—discussion, making notes, and using two- and three-dimensional forms of representation—are part of learning about things in the children's environment and not simply ways of making a neat written record, graph, diagram, or model or giving a verbal report.

In relation to discussion, points made throughout the book have been brought together to underscore the value of discussion in all science activities. The result of explaining ideas and putting them together with others' gives each child a richer supply of ideas than he or she could obtain alone. The discussion continues the learning process and creates a report on what has been found. The discussion that takes place in different situations serves different purposes:

- whole-class discussion is the arena for sharing ideas that groups have already talked through and are prepared to support with evidence
- discussion in small groups with a teacher present gives the teacher a chance to challenge children's ideas and offer some alternatives for them to consider
- discussion among a small group of children alone helps them to try out ideas that are still in a somewhat unformed state and lets them hear a variety of ideas from others

In relation to personal written communication, children should become accustomed to using a notebook (sometimes aided by a tape recorder) for jotting down observations during activities. It has been suggested that these notes should be regarded as personal to the child, not ones to be "marked" or graded by the teacher. The role of the teacher is to help children find more efficient and effective ways of keeping notes and records, by introducing suggestions at times about when these can be used. A delicate balance is required, for too much guidance too soon can lead to children recording what they think the teacher wants them to put down and the results they think they should get. Some suggestions have been given for helping children to use better techniques and appropriate words without over-direction. The resulting notes and records are the children's own; valuable to them as aide-mémoire and valuable to the teacher as a source of information about children's thinking.

Nonverbal representations, in the form of drawings, models, and paintings, have their role in learning science. The purpose of producing the representation must be clear to the teacher and the children. Drawing will not necessarily improve observation unless it is preceded by some discussion of what might be relevant for the particular purpose of the drawing, and followed by a discussion in which certain features of the object are compared with the representation. Teachers should ensure that children are introduced to various techniques they might want to use in their representations and have some practice of relevant skills. Examples have been given of how children's preconceptions influence their drawing, paintings, and models. It follows that studying these products can give a useful pointer to teachers as to how children believe things to be.

Suggestions for actions the teacher can take to help the development of these forms of communication follow:

Encouraging discussion

1. When children are working in groups, make it clear that you expect them to discuss with each other and to try to settle differences by finding evidence for one view or another.

2. Only start a discussion with children in small groups when they have something to tell you or to consult you about; if they are purposefully working on their own, leave them to it.
3. Find out the children's own ideas about a problem on which they want your help before offering your own; take part in discussing the problem as a member of the group as far as possible.
4. Give five or ten minutes' warning before a whole-class discussion so that groups can prepare themselves for reporting.
5. In a whole-class discussion, make sure each group has its say on a topic before going on to another one.
6. Accept all points for consideration and let the children object to findings or ideas that don't fit in with their own; the disputed areas should be identified for further work.

Helping children to keep records

1. Provide children with a notebook that they can use in their own way to keep some kind of record of their activities.
2. In group discussions, ask children to use their notes to recall what they have done, so that they see the value of keeping a record.
3. Read through the notebooks occasionally, without correcting them but suggesting words or ways of organizing the information that will make the records more useful.

Helping children to use drawing, painting, and modeling

1. Discuss with children the purpose of making a drawing, painting, or model before they embark on it, so that they focus on relevant features and ways of representing them.
2. Sometimes allow a free choice of materials and techniques for representation; at other times discuss the appropriateness of various possibilities beforehand.
3. Ensure that children have at some time practised the techniques and know the range in the use of materials available to them.
4. Discuss the products but don't judge them; show interest in discrepancies between the representation and the object and the children's reasons for them.

5. Study children's representations; notice what they treat in detail, what only cursorily, what they ignore, what they change. This will help in understanding what interests them and how they interpret what they see.

Chapter 9

Assessing for Learning

Our concern here is using assessment to help children's learning. To those who associate, or may equate, the word *assessment* with testing, this may not make sense, or at any rate, not seem a high priority. So we have to start by clarifying the meaning we attach to it here. Assessment serves different functions in education and so we discuss its purpose in helping learning in the context of other purposes. Being clear about what we don't mean is central to knowing what we do mean. We also want to make clear that there are some very strong reasons for giving attention to assessment for learning; it leads to improved learning of the kind that we are concerned with in this book. After summarizing these reasons we look at what is involved in practice, both for the teacher and the children.

Meanings and Purposes

Assessment—or evaluation—or testing—although not identical, all involve gathering information about children's ideas and skills and making judgments for various purposes. In primary school classrooms the main purposes relating to children's learning are

- to find out where children are in the development of desired ideas, skills, and attitudes in order to decide the next steps that will help them in this development (we call this assessment *for* learning, or formative assessment)
- to find out what children have achieved at certain points in order to monitor progress from time to time and to report on achievement

to parents and others with an interest in the children's education (we call this assessment *of* learning or summative assessment)

It is with formative assessment that we are chiefly concerned here, but since more effort and attention is often given to summative assessment we must discuss this too. The difference between the two lies not so much in the way they are carried out but in the use that is made of the information that they provide. Both formative assessment and summative assessment *can* involve information gathered by teachers, but formative assessment can *only* serve its purpose if it uses this information gathered in this way—for it cannot otherwise serve its purpose. Conversely, just because information is gathered by teachers this does not make the assessment formative. It is only formative when the information is used to decide the appropriate next steps for individual children and to adapt teaching accordingly. In some cases the focus is the individual child and in some cases the whole class.

Formative assessment

For the individual child, formative assessment occurs in this kind of way:

> Ten-year-old Martyn was trying to set up a circuit so that his group could operate an electric bell from a switch. He had successfully connected the bell to the switch but placed the battery on the same arm of the switch so that it rang continuously. His arrangement is shown in Figure 9–1. The teacher watched this and then asked him to trace with his fingers the path from the battery around to the bell and back again. Because this went through part of the switch, Martyn thought he had done what was required. The teacher thought that it was possible that he had not connected this primitive switch with the familiar switch that turns lights on and off. So she left the bell aside for a while to give him chance to explore the switch, for it was clear that he did not identify it as just a way of making and breaking a circuit nor realize the effect this had on the components of a circuit. Had the teacher just told him to connect a wire to the other side of the switch, or if he had done this either by chance or by seeing what others were doing, he would have succeeded in using the switch to operate the bell but still would not have understood the main purpose of the activity, which was to apply and extend his understanding of an electric circuit.

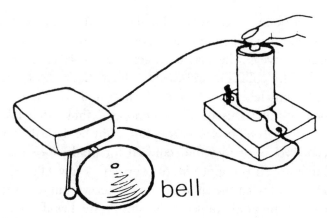

Figure 9–1.

For the whole class, a good example is another teacher at an early stage of a lesson on simple circuits with her third-grade class:

> The children had spent about twenty minutes working in pairs to try to make a bulb light from a simple cell. To bring their ideas together she asked each pair to draw on the white board the circuits they had tried, putting ones that worked in one place and ones that didn't in another. She went on to ask the children to pick out circuits they were not sure about and to try to reproduce the circuit drawings with the equipment. In this way the children identified the errors in their drawings and the teacher identified their misunderstandings. She explained after the lesson that she had two main purposes in mind: "One of the reasons that the students were putting drawings up on the board was for them to see the importance of including detail in their drawings and also I can take a quick look up there and get a read on basically where the class is as a whole. Some need some help." Her use of the white board was a device that gave her a quick overview of the children's early progress toward grasping the essentials of a circuit and enabled her to make a judgment as to whether to move on or give more time for this early exploration. (Linda Block, WGBH video 1997)

Summative assessment

Summative assessment provides a summary of what has been achieved at a certain time. It can take the form of a review of each child's work across the period of time in question, perhaps collected in a portfolio, or it can take the form of a test, or it can be some combination of summarized work and a test score. The key word here is *summarized* for, to serve its purpose, summative assessment has to be in a form that concisely conveys what has been achieved. It cannot convey all the details that are collected and used for formative assessment since this would be unwieldy, perhaps confusing, and for these reasons would probably not be used. The "summary" thus often takes the form of a grade or level or score. A child might be described as having achieved level X or met the standard for grade Y or reached a score of Z in a test. It is important, of course, to know what X, Y, and Z mean in terms of what the child can do, or knows, but too often this is forgotten and the grade or score becomes reified as if it had some existence and meaning in its own right.

Summative assessment can also be used for the purpose of providing information about individual children or about a whole class. For the individual child, parents and other teachers need information about individuals—and hopefully they receive more than the terse level or grade. The use of information about the whole class for the purpose of evaluating a teacher or school is controversial, but nevertheless widespread. When information about children's performance is used in this way—often made public and possibly used to influence resource allocation—it becomes "high stakes." Further, the more important the consequences of children's results for the status, reputation, and support of the school, the more attention is given to ensuring that the measurements of children's achievement are "fair." This may lead to a preference for basing results on tests, since these are traditionally regarded as being more reliable than teachers' judgments (even though there is little real evidence to support this view). The tests of greatest reliability are those that focus narrowly on questions with well-defined "right" answers so that they can be reliably graded. But the more reliable they are, the less they say about the full range of goals of education. When the results of these tests become high stakes it is inevitable that teaching focuses on the knowledge that is tested. What we end up with is teaching children to pass tests rather than teaching them science.

Is there anything that can be done to avoid the impact of tests having a stranglehold on the curriculum? The answer is hopeful. Levels of achievement can be raised in another, more educationally sound, way. Although teachers' own assessments tend to be downgraded and even snuffed out by high-stakes testing, there is convincing evidence that using formative assessment to help learning not only preserves the kind of learning we have been concerned to enhance in this book—that is, building understanding through the active engagement of children with materials and with ideas from others—but indeed leads to improved attainment as measured by tests required by national, state, or local systems. This applies, of course, to all classrooms whether or not in the grip of a testing regime. In the next section we look at these arguments and the supporting evidence.

Why Formative Assessment?

Since the purpose of formative assessment is to help learning, one of the strong reasons for developing practice in formative assessment starts from considering learning. In Chapter 1 (page 11) we described a framework for learning through inquiry. Looking back at that we see that children are *using* their ideas and skills at many points. But whether they are *developing* their ideas and skills depends upon the extent to which both the children and the teacher have identified, and are working for, progress in these aspects of learning science. By finding what ideas the children bring to try to understand a new experience, the teacher is in a position to ensure that these are taken into account—tested if necessary—so that any new ideas, or modification of existing ones, make sense to the children. By noticing how they make their observations, express their predictions, and plan their investigations, the teacher can see where the children are in the development of these skills, and he or she is in a position to decide if they need help to do these things more scientifically. Similar opportunities arise when it comes to the important step of interpreting and seeing how their findings help them answer their original question.

We can see that at all these stages the action the teacher takes can be informed by what the children do or say or write or draw. If this information is not taken into account, then the steps the teacher requires the children to take may be out of their reach and they have to follow blindly. Alternatively the steps may be too small, leaving children unchallenged and missing opportunities for learning. This is not to say that in every part of every activity the teacher has to be gathering information and making teaching decisions on the spot, which would be impossible. What it does mean is having a clear view of progression in learning and making sure that relevant information about where children are in this progression is picked up during the regular course of interactions with children.

Now we turn to the second important reason for improving the practice of formative assessment. This comes from looking across an extensive range of research studies about the effect of classroom assessment. When Black and Wiliam reviewed these studies in 1997, they identified strikingly clear evidence that formative assessment is a most significant element in raising the achievement of students and especially that of the lower-achieving students. The effects on achievement were indeed large, much greater than changes that can be brought about by changes in other conditions, including reducing class size (Black and Wiliam 1998). The characteristics of classroom practice associated with these gains in learning were:

- that assessment was used by teachers to adapt teaching
- that teachers gave feedback to children in terms of how to improve their work, not in terms of judgmental comments, grades, or marks
- that children were actively engaged in learning—meaning that they were active in developing their understanding, not passively receiving information
- that children were engaged in self-assessment and in helping to decide their next steps
- that teachers regarded all children as being capable of learning

The potential for helping children to learn more effectively is very great if these classroom conditions can be brought about. Some of these conditions are not new—good teachers have always practiced them intuitively. However, by looking more closely at what they involve we may be able to spread this practice more widely.

Using Assessment to Adapt Teaching

Formative assessment involves teachers in gathering information, interpreting it in terms of progress toward goals, deciding the next steps that need to be taken, and then helping children to take these steps. Although these separate components of the process can be identified in theory, in practice they will often occur at much the same time as each other.

Gathering and interpreting information

A number of ways of gathering information as part of teaching have been mentioned in earlier chapters:

- questioning (pages 31, 57)
- asking children to draw their ideas (pages 58, 114)
- concept maps (page 59)
- discussing words (page 58)
- listening to children-only discussions (pages 58, 104)
- and, more generally, observing what children do as well as looking at what they produce

Observing actions is of particular value for gathering evidence about children's developing process skills and attitudes. But it helps if you know what to look for. As we saw in Chapter 7, observation for anyone—child, teacher, or scientist—involves knowing what to look for, otherwise you might miss it. Teachers have found it particularly helpful to have in mind the kinds of things that children do or say that are indicators of a skill, attitude, or idea being used. If, at the same time, these "indicators" are arranged in a sequence that reflects progression in development of these attributes, then they help also in the interpretation of the children's behavior and give some pointers to the next steps. Here are some examples (from Harlen 2000a), for planning, observing, and communicating:

Planning investigations

Do the children:

1. start with a useful general approach even if details are lacking or need further thought?
2. identify the variable that has to be changed and the things that should be kept the same for a fair test?
3. identify what to look for what or measure to obtain a result in an investigation?

4. succeed in planning a fair test using a given framework of questions?
5. compare their actual procedures after the event with what was planned?
6. spontaneously structure their plans so that independent, dependent, and controlled variables are identified and steps taken to ensure that the results obtained are as accurate as they can reasonably be?

Observing

Do the children:

1. succeed in identifying obvious differences and similarities between objects and materials?
2. make use of several senses in exploring objects or materials?
3. identify differences of detail between objects or materials?
4. identify points of similarity between objects where differences are more obvious than similarities?
5. use their senses appropriately and extend the range of sight using a hand lens or microscope as necessary?
6. distinguish from many observations those that are relevant to the problem in hand?

Communicating

Do the children:

1. talk freely about their activities and the ideas they have, with or without making a written record?
2. listen to others' ideas and look at their results?
3. use drawings, writing, models, paintings to present their ideas and findings?
4. use tables, graphs, and charts when these are suggested to record and organize results?
5. regularly and spontaneously use information books to check or supplement their investigations?
6. choose a form for recording or presenting results that is both considered and justified in relation to the type of information and the audience?

In each of these lists the questions refer to behaviors indicating progression, from 1 to 6, in the particular skill. They were created from the best of what is known about development in general, but they will not fit each and every child exactly. They have several uses. Initially they prompt teachers to observe particularly relevant aspects of children's behavior. Then they help in bringing together observations made over time to address the questions for each child. In this way they help the teacher to find where the answers turn from "yes" into "sometimes" into "no." Where it becomes difficult to say yes or no indicates the child's position in the progression, where skills need to be consolidated before moving toward the ones where there is a definite "no."

The same approach can be used for scientific attitudes, for example:

Respect for evidence

Do the children:

1. attempt to justify conclusions in terms of evidence even if the interpretation is influenced by preconceived ideas?
2. realize when the evidence doesn't fit a conclusion based on expectations, although they may challenge the evidence rather than the conclusion?
3. check parts of the evidence that don't fit an overall pattern or conclusions?
4. accept only interpretations or conclusions for which there is supporting evidence?
5. show a desire to collect further evidence to check conclusions before accepting them?
6. recognize that no conclusion is so firm that it can't be challenged by further evidence?

When it comes to children's understanding, the emphasis is upon children's ability to use progressively more complex concepts relating to particular "big ideas." For example:

Forces and movement

Can the children use these ideas?

1. To make anything move or stop moving there has to be something pushing, pulling, or twisting it.
2. Speed is a way of saying how far something moves in a certain time.
3. How quickly an object will start moving depends on the amount of force acting on it, and the faster it is moving the more force is needed to stop it.
4. It takes more force to start or stop a heavy object than a lighter one.
5. Things fall because of a force acting on everything on the Earth pulling toward the Earth (gravity).
6. When several forces act on an object their effect is combined.
7. When an object is not moving, the forces acting on it cancel each other, and there must be a force acting against gravity to stop it falling (as in floating).

Helping children to take the next steps

The test of whether the assessment is or is not formative is whether it is used to take children forward in their learning. It is of little value to know where children are unless this informs teaching. So what can teachers do to help children? We noted in Chapter 5 in the discussion of helping children's concept development that we can't be prescriptive about what to do in any particular case since this must depend on the ideas that are revealed. But we can propose a number of strategies. An important part of deciding which is appropriate in a particular case is to identify how children have come to their ideas. This generally indicates whether they will benefit most from more exploration, a wider range of experience, testing their ideas, talking through them, or trying alternative ideas with scaffolding from the teacher (see page 62).

In relation to the development of process skills there are some general points that emerge from the discussion of separate skills in Chapters 6, 7, and 8. Teachers can help children to develop their process skills by:

- providing opportunity to use process skills in the exploration of materials and phenomena at first hand
- asking questions that require children to use the process skills
- involving children in critically reviewing how they have carried out their activities

- small-group and whole-class discussion of whether their ideas are consistent with the evidence
- discussing how they have learned as well as what they have learned (metacognition)
- teaching the techniques needed for advancing skills

Feedback from Teacher to Children

Feedback from the teacher is an important vehicle for enabling children to know how to improve their work, but its effectiveness depends on the form of the feedback. Often teachers give feedback on how well something has been done using a mark, grade, or a judgmental comment. Research evidence supports the experience of effective and sensitive teachers that giving marks or grades does not improve learning. What *does* improve both interest and achievement is giving comments that are nonjudgmental and that indicate how improvements can be made. Giving marks or grades together with comments is just as ineffective as giving marks or grades only, since the students' attention is focused on how well they did and the comments are ignored. Only those with high marks feel good, and the others feel that they have been labeled as "no good." This is consistent with Kohn's (1993) telling dictum:

"Never grade students while they are still learning."

Because this point is so important in characterizing feedback that is formative, it is worth spelling out what is nonjudgmental and what is judgmental. Nonjudgmental feedback gives information and

- focuses on the task, not the person;
- encourages children to think about the work, not about their feelings or ability;
- provides comments on what to do next and ideas about how to do it.

Judgmental feedback:

- is expressed in terms of how well the child has done, rather than the quality of the work that has been done
- gives a judgment that encourages children to label themselves

- provides a grade or mark that children use often to compare themselves with each other or with what they want to achieve

It is useful to note that praise comes into the judgmental category; it makes children feel they are doing well but does not necessarily help them to do better. (So praise is fine if you want to make children feel good, but not if you want them to improve their work.) A remark or mark that indicates a judgment on the work will divert children's attention from any comment that is made about improvement. Children are more motivated by comments that help them think about their work and realize what they can do to improve it, and that give them help in doing this. This means oral or written questions and comments such as, "How did you decide which was the best _____ ?" "Is there another way of explaining this by thinking of what happened when _____ ?" "Next time, imagine that someone else is going to use your drawing to set up the circuit and make sure that you show them clearly what to do."

Children Assessing Their Own Work

Several of the key factors in effective formative assessment relate to children taking an active role in their learning. This includes taking part in assessing their own progress and in helping to decide their next steps and what they need to do to take them. All these things put children "in the know" about their learning. They don't then have to rely on someone else telling them how they are doing and what to do next; they are in a position to take some responsibility for their own learning. But this does not come about without sustained consistent action from the teacher that involves:

- sharing with children the goal of learning in an activity so that they know where they are going
- giving children some way of judging where they are in relation to this goal
- helping them to think about their learning (metacognition again)
- ensuring that the children have the skills and confidence to take the next steps

All of these are important and none is easy to implement, but they all depend on the first one, sharing with children the goals of their learning. That is the place to start if a teacher wants to move toward "letting children in on their learning." Anyone who is trying to learn needs a clear idea of what he or she is aiming for and children are no exception. This includes both goals that refer to the kind of thing to do and those referring to doing it well. However, it is not easy to communicate learning goals to children and this certainly can't be done in the formal language of "targets" and "standards." Some ways in which teachers have succeeded in sharing their goals with children are by discussing "best work"; stating its purpose at the start of an activity and reinforcing during the course of it; asking children to show what they have learned; and using examples.

Discussing "best work"

One teacher described an approach that can be used with children from about the age of eight. It begins with the children selecting their "best" work and collecting it in a folder or bag. Children are given time to review and select their work; time is also set aside for the teacher to talk to each child about why certain pieces of work have been selected. During this discussion the way in which the children are judging the quality of their work becomes clear. The children's reasons may have messages for the teacher. For example, if work seems to be selected less for its content than for its tidy appearance, then perhaps this aspect is being overemphasized.

At first the discussion serves to clarify the criteria the children use for selecting work as their best. "Tell me what you particularly liked about this piece of work." Gradually it will be possible for the teacher to suggest criteria without dictating what the children should be selecting. This can be done through comments on the work. "That was a very good way of showing your results, I could see at a glance which came out best." "I'm glad you think that was your best investigation because although you didn't get the result you expected, you did it very carefully and made sure that the result was fair."

Discussing the purpose of activities

Another example is the teacher who regularly discusses with the children the purpose of their activities, so that they know where to focus their attention. Although she usually does this in general terms with the whole class at the start, this is never enough on its own. She reinforces it in her discussions with groups later and may identify more specific targets to suit individual children. It is important to find the right wording that shares the goal without telling children "the answer." In science this is more difficult than in some other subjects (where, for instance, the teacher could indicate that the goal of a particular piece of writing was to use quotation marks correctly). For example, in explaining the goal of an investigation, the goal should not be put in the form "Find out that [stating the intended idea]" but rather "Find out about [the materials to be used]." When the goal is to refine the process of inquiry, the children should be aware of this and not be left with the impression that they have spent all their time finding out something that is in fact rather trivial. This happened in a class where some boys were observed to have spent three lessons finding out which of three kinds of paper was the strongest. The observer interviewed the boys after the lesson:

INTERVIEWER: What do you think you have learned from doing your investigation?

ROBERT: . . . that graph paper is stronger, that green one.

INTERVIEWER: Right, is that it?

ROBERT: Um . . .

INTERVIEWER: You spent three lessons doing that, seems a long time to spend finding out that graph paper is stronger.

JAMES: Yeah, and we also found out which . . . paper is stronger. Not just the graph paper, all of them.

The boys appeared to be unaware of the process of investigation as a learning goal, in contrast with their teacher. It seems reasonable to assume that, had they been aware of this goal, they would have reflected more on the way they were investigating, found more satisfaction in the investigation, and made more progress toward the goal that the teacher had in mind but kept to herself.

Asking children to show what they have learned

Children can be asked to show others what they have learned. At times when they report the findings of their inquiries to the whole class this is an opportunity to ask them to include a statement of what they have learned as well as what they did and found out. Particularly when there was some unplanned exploration or problem that had to be solved, the teacher can ask, "What did you learn from that?"

One teacher set the children to make a practical test for each other to test their knowledge of simple circuits. The tasks were far harder than the teacher would have given. All the children, those setting and responding to the tasks, not only enjoyed this challenge but extended their learning in the process.

Using examples

Communicating the intended quality, or standard, of work to aim for is difficult at any level. Teachers find it helpful to have standards exemplified by children's work and in a similar way these are also helpful to children. Indeed there is no reason why some of the examples produced for teachers in publications such as *Performance Standards: New Standards* (1997) or *Exemplification of Standards: Science at Key Stages 1 and 2, Levels 1 to 5* (SCAA 1995) should not be shared with children, to show what other children have done. This can avoid problems that might arise by discussing examples taken from the work of classmates. Sometimes it is useful not to have a perfect example but to discuss shortcomings as well as the more positive aspects of a piece of work. A collection of pieces of work could be created for this purpose but it is best if the authors of the work cannot be identified. Teachers from different schools can often agree to exchange examples of work for this purpose.

Of course, involving children in assessing their own work takes time, but this time is paid back severalfold by the children's efforts, their enjoyment in learning, the reduction in waiting time (because they don't have to wait for the teacher to tell them what to do by), and the focusing of effort where it is most needed.

Summary of Main Points

This chapter has been concerned with assessment for the two main purposes that it has in the primary or elementary school: formative and summative. Formative assessment is part of teaching and can provide information to adapt teaching according to the needs and progress of the children. It is a process in which teachers gather detailed information about all learning goals and use this to identify next steps for individual children or for the class as a whole.

The purpose of summative assessment is to provide a summary of what has been achieved at a certain time. It often takes the form of a test but can also be based on summarizing across a range of children's work. When summative assessment is used for evaluating and judging teachers and schools for high-stakes purposes, there is a tendency for the tests to be narrowed to increase reliability and, in turn, to influence the curriculum and teaching.

The improvement of formative assessment can raise standards of achievement of all children and particularly the lower achievers. The potential improvement is greater than for any other intervention in children's education.

Formative assessment is most effective when teachers use it to adapt teaching, provide nonjudgmental feedback to children, involve children in self-assessment and making decisions about their next steps, and engage all children in active learning. The following are suggestions for actions that teachers can take in relation to these key components of formative assessment:

Feedback into teaching

1. Collect information as part of regular interaction with children, ensuring that there is evidence for the judgments that are made.
2. Interpret the information in terms of what it means for progression in the development of concepts, skills, and attitudes.
3. Use the information about where children are in their development to decide the next steps possible for them to take and the appropriate strategy for helping them to take these steps.

Feedback to children

1. Comment on the work, not on the ability or performance of the child.
2. Indicate by question or comment what the child should do either to improve the work or to move on.
3. Do not give marks or grades even if these are accompanied by a comment.

Involving children in self-assessment

1. Tell children what they should be aiming to try to do in an activity but without suggesting a particular outcome.
2. Ask them what they have learned from an activity and what they have still to learn.
3. Help the children to identify good work, through discussing their own work and examples of others' work.
4. Involve them in deciding what their next steps should be and how they might set about taking them.

References

Association for Science Education (ASE). 1998a. *ASE Guide to Primary Science Education*. Cheltenham, UK: Stanley Thornes.
———. 1998b. *Primary Science 56*.
Barnes, D. 1976. *From Communication to Curriculum*. Harmondsworth, UK: Penguin.
Bell, B. F. 1981. "When Is an Animal Not an Animal?" *Journal of Biological Education* 15 (3): 213–18.
Biddulph, F., and R. J. Osborne. 1984. "Pupils' Ideas About Floating and Sinking." *Research in Science Education* (14): 114–24.
Black, P. J., and D. Wiliam. 1998. "Assessment and Classroom Learning." *Assessment in Education* 5 (1): 7–74.
Deci, E. L., and R. M. Ryan. 1985. *Intrinsic Motivation and Self-Determination in Human Behavior*. New York: Plenum Press.
Freyberg, P. S., R. J. Osborne, and C. R. Tasker. 1983. "The Learning in Science Project." In *New Trends in Primary School Science Education*, edited by W. Harlen. Paris: UNESCO.
Harlen, W. 2000a. *Teaching, Learning, and Assessing Science 5–12*. London: Paul Chapman Publishing.
———. 2000b. *The Teaching of Science in Primary Schools*. London: David Fulton Publishing.
Harlen, W., C. Macro, M. Schilling, D. Malvern, and K. Reed. 1990. *Progress in Primary Science*. London: Routledge.
Harlen, W., and S. Jelly. 1997. *Developing Science in the Primary Classroom*. Harlow, Essex, UK: Longman.
Kohn, A. 1993. *Punished by Rewards*. Boston: Houghton Mifflin.
McMeniman, M. 1989. "Motivation to Learn." In *Educational Psychology: An Australian Perspective*, edited by P. Langford. Sydney: Longman.
National Center on Education and the Economy and the University of Pittsburgh. 1997. *Performance Standards: New Standards*, Vol. 1, Elementary Science. National Center on Education and the Economy and the University of Pittsburgh.

Naylor, S., and B. Keogh. 2000. *Concept Cartoons in Science Education.* Crewe, Cheshire, UK: Millgate House Publishers.

Ormerod, M. B., and D. Duckworth. 1975. *Pupils' Attitudes to Science.* Windsor, UK: NFER.

Osborne, R. J. 1983. "Towards Modifying Children's Ideas About Electric Current." *Journal of Research in Science and Technological Education* 1: 73–82.

Osborne, R. J., and P. Freyberg. 1982. Learning in Science (Forms 1–4) Final Report. Hamilton, NZ: Science Education Research Unit, University of Waikato, Hamilton, New Zealand.

———. 1985. *Learning in Science: The Implications of "Children's Science."* London: Heinemann.

SCAA. 1995. *Exemplification of Standards: Science at Key Stages 1 and 2, Levels 1 to 5.* London: Schools Curriculum and Assessment Authority.

Science 5–13. 1972. *Working with Wood.* Unit for Teachers. London: Macdonald.

SPACE Research Reports. 1990. *Growth.* Liverpool, UK: University of Liverpool Press.

———. 1990. *Light.* Liverpool, UK: University of Liverpool Press.

Tunnicliffe, S. 2001. "Apples: Children's Observational and Imaginary Drawings." *Primary Science Review* 69.

WGBH Video. 1997. *Completing the Circuit.*

Index